A "Very Special" Tale of Faith, Hope, & Hand Sanitizer

A "Very Special" Tale of Faith, Hope, & Hand Sanitizer

BRANDON L. BOSWELL

A "VERY SPECIAL" TALE OF FAITH, HOPE, & HAND SANITIZER

iUniverse books may be ordered through booksellers or by contacting:

iUniverse
1663 Liberty Drive
Bloomington, IN 47403
www.iuniverse.com
844-349-9409

Because of the dynamic nature of the Internet, any web addresses or links contained in this book may have changed since publication and may no longer be valid. The views expressed in this work are solely those of the author and do not necessarily reflect the views of the publisher, and the publisher hereby disclaims any responsibility for them.

Any people depicted in stock imagery provided by Getty Images are models, and such images are being used for illustrative purposes only.
Certain stock imagery © Getty Images.

Scripture quotations marked KJV are from the Holy Bible, King James Version (Authorized Version). First published in 1611. Quoted from the KJV Classic Reference Bible, Copyright © 1983 by The Zondervan Corporation.

Scripture quotations marked NIV are taken from the Holy Bible, New International Version®. NIV®. Copyright © 1973, 1978, 1984 by International Bible Society. Used by permission of Zondervan. All rights reserved. Biblica

ISBN: 978-1-6632-6290-5 (sc)
ISBN: 978-1-6632-6289-9 (e)

Library of Congress Control Number: 2024909802

Print information available on the last page.

iUniverse rev. date: 05/15/2024

For Mom, Dad, & Sis

A-B-C-L-I-F-E

(INTRODUCTION)

As I write the introduction to this book, I'm actually reminded of my previous book, *You'll Laugh a Little, You'll Cry a Little.* Had I known what the contents of this book would be, I would have been wise to save that title for this one instead for reasons that will become clear soon enough.

Writing that previous book was like being at home one day, when, all of a sudden, I have a craving for a big bowl of ice cream. So, I mosey on over to the fridge, open the door to the freezer, and find that desired carton of ice cream I had been saving for a special occasion. These days, a special occasion is any day I wake up in the morning. If I have the courage to get out of bed and interact with the rest of humanity, then it's a *really* special occasion. Setting the bar low makes for far more special occasions.

So, by now, I take out the ice cream and set it on the counter. I know it will be one of my two favorite flavors: "Mint Chocolate Chip on My Shoulder" or "That's the

Final Straw!-berry" (the two most popular flavors for us Baptists.)

I peel back the lid on the carton and discover there is just enough ice cream left for one last good-sized bowl. I walk over to the silverware drawer, take out the largest spoon I can find and place it next to the largest bowl I can find. I then begin scooping every last bit of ice cream out of the carton and into the bowl. I'm so hungry I also scrape the ice cream off the bottom of the lid. With detailed precision, I even retrieve the remaining bits of any chips or bits that have stubbornly stuck to the side of the carton. I look like someone trying to remove a tick from the underside of a chihuahua without losing a finger.

When I'm done, I stare at the bowl of ice cream in front of me. I'm grinning from ear-to-ear because I know this is going to taste *amazing*. I soon devour every last bit of ice cream in the bowl and think to myself, *Life is good!*

And, for awhile, life *is* good … until the day comes when I want another bowl of ice cream. So, I return to the freezer, open it up, only to then realize that I already ate the last of the ice cream and never replaced it.

Life isn't so good after all.

Thankfully, when the time was right, God spoke to my heart. Actually, He spoke to my stomach. Like I said,

I'm Baptist, and God speaks where He knows I'm most likely to listen. So, God told me to get up and look in the freezer one more time just to see what was in there. I wasn't optimistic, but reluctantly, I made the journey.

Unlike my previous trip to the freezer, this time, I dug a bit deeper. (In my freezer, trying to find a certain item is similar to going on an archaeological expedition.) Amazingly, in the back corner, behind a bag of frozen okra and under a box of frozen pizza, I made the life-changing discovery: another carton of ice cream I forgot was in there! I open it up and, thankfully, there is just enough ice cream left for another bowl. There's a bit of freezer burn, but I convince myself it's just added protein that makes this a healthier dessert option. There may not be as much ice cream as I wanted, but it's more than enough to fill my appetite.

Just like a search for more ice cream, when it comes to writing, sometimes you just have to dig a little deeper to come up with ideas for the next book. However, if you're "hungry" enough, it's well worth the effort.

* * *

For over fifteen years, I have humbly worked in the retail service industry. At one time I would have said "proudly" worked, but after my first three minutes on the job, I was quickly humbled and have remained as such. When I tell this to other people who work in retail, the usual response is, "Three minutes? Were you late clocking in?"

When I reached the BIG 1-5, I was awarded what I jokingly called "my stupid little" fifteen year service certificate. Truthfully though, I wanted that dumb piece of paper. I worked hard for that certificate. I have it sitting in my bedroom as we speak and plan to get it framed. I'm not going to the first Dollar General I come to and buy the first frame I find either, no sir. This is a *big* occasion. I'm planning a trip to Five Below. No expense will be spared.

In the months leading up to my anniversary, I was afraid something would keep me from making it to fifteen years and earning my certificate. As a precaution, I took time to figure out how many protected paid days off I had at my disposal in case I needed to use them. It's similar to what many of us did back in school when we had a tough course and we used a calculator and sheet of paper with all our grades to figure out what our lowest grade on the final exam could be and still pass the course. Ironically, if many of us had made the same effort studying as we did figuring out what our lowest grade could be, we wouldn't have had to worry about failing. I'm no exception.

The thought of summer school terrified me as a kid. I had no desire to see any of my teachers before the fall (when school is *supposed* to start). The fear of seeing a teacher at their desk in July was as bad as a groom seeing his bride in her wedding gown just before the ceremony. I thought it would lead to bad luck and a lifetime of misery.

I actually ended up doing two "tours of duty" in summer school back in college when I got a bit behind taking a couple of developmental math courses. Honestly, summer school wasn't all that bad. It was much more laid back than the fall or spring semesters. On more than one occasion, the teacher didn't make us do certain assignments they normally had their students do at other times in the school year simply because there just wasn't enough time. I remember thinking, *Wow, had I known summer school would be this great, I would have become a slacker ages ago.* Sadly, by then it was too late and I had long since developed a solid work ethic.

Speaking of work, I should mention that despite all my trials and tribulations of working with the general public, sometimes they have provided me with story ideas for my books. If I can't think of anything good to write about, I can rest assured knowing that as soon I'm back at work for my next shift, I'll almost assuredly hear some great stories. Sometimes, I even become *part* of the stories.

There was the time I had to intervene when a group of customers started arguing over something. One female customer got so frustrated with a male customer that she told him he *needed* Jesus. Then, another female customer decided to throw her hat into the ring and also told the male customer that he *needed* Jesus.

You hear stories about spontaneous acts of spiritual revival breaking out, but I don't think this is quite what they mean. If this was a revival, then I felt like I was being held against my will in a tent meeting with Jerry Springer as the guest evangelist. Thankfully, I already have Jesus. What I needed right then was a *really* strong painkiller.

There was also the time I needed to get the attention of a group of customers. I walked up and said, "Excuse me, folks." Well, one customer didn't appreciate me doing this. In fact, they took offense to it. Why, you may ask? Well, the customer was upset because I had referred to them and their group as "folks" and considered the word "folks" to be offensive. I always knew the day could come when I would get into trouble at work for using the "f-word," but this wasn't quite how I imagined it going down. I won't go into how it ended, but I will say that customer and I didn't exchange addresses and we're not on each others Christmas card list. I hope that customer never reads this book. I don't think they would appreciate my folksy style of humor anyway. (Oops, I used the "f-word" again. Pardon my language.)

Conversations with co-workers are also an amazing source of story ideas. Not long ago, a co-worker friend named Victoria shared with me about how the phone system in our store hadn't been working properly. Many of the customer's calls were being rerouted to her department, which happened to be our in-store pharmacy. She told me she was getting tired of answering questions about wedding cakes and tires. I suggested that the next time someone calls and asks about wedding cakes, she should suggest that for a wedding cake no one will *ever* forget, they should instead purchase three tires, each one smaller than the other. Then, stack the tires on top of each other from largest to smallest, cover the tires with cake frosting, and place a little bride and groom on the top. At the reception when the bride and groom go to cut the "cake," everyone will be in for what I'm sure will become a cherished memory in the decades to come. Since Victoria is still employed, though, it's safe to assume she has yet to implement my suggestion. (By the way, if a bride and groom end up chewing rubber tires together on their wedding day, is that considered good luck? Perhaps if it's a "Goodyear" tire.)

* * *

Recently at work, I overheard a conversation between two women, both mothers of young children. One woman was telling the other one about an experience she had with her daughter, who was around the age of three. I can't recall exactly how the story went, but the way I tell it is funnier so we'll go with my version: The woman and her daughter were riding together in the family car. The daughter, like a lot of young kids, wanted to get her mother's attention. If you're a mom reading this, you'll probably know how she set out to do this. If you guessed by exclaiming, "Mama! Mama! Mama!" over and over, you win the prize. (Sadly, that prize isn't noise-canceling headphones. Sorry.)

Now, at this point I think it's safe to assume that this mother, like any mother of a young child who is trying desperately to cling to her sanity, was wishing her daughter would pipe down and let her drive in peace. However, as any mom would tell you, the magical genies that grant such wishes are few and far between these days. To find them, you would likely have to take a trip to a Disney theme park. To do that would mean having that same child in the backseat shouting, "Mama! Mama! Mama!" now followed by, "Are we there yet?! Are we there yet?! Are we there yet?!" You have to wonder if the benefits outweigh the costs.

Regardless, the mother was doing her best to concentrate behind the wheel as her daughter continued chanting her "mama mantra." Finally, the poor mother, somewhat agitated, asked her daughter, "What is it??"

The daughter's response: "Mama ... A is for apple!"

The End.

I'm pretty sure at this point the mom looked at her daughter and said or wanted to say something along the lines of, "Well, good to know. Now, hush up, Mama's trying not to drive us through the Pearly Gates right now!"

It was honestly a cute story the way she told it. If I had been the parent in this story, it wouldn't have been as cute. Now, I'm not a parent, I'm single, and I don't even drive a car. I was born legally blind and don't drive, making the roads (and sidewalks, too) a little safer for us all.

However, for the sake of my page count, let's say I could drive and was a parent of a young child and faced this exact situation. Here's how it would have likely turned out:

Kid: "Daddy! Daddy! Daddy!"

Me: (Ignoring the kid for as long as humanly possible)

Kid: "Daddy! Daddy! Daddy!"

Me: (Giving up) "WHAT IS IT!?? I'm trying to drive in heavy traffic here! What is so important??!!"

Kid: "Daddy … A is for apple!"

Me: "Well, good to know! You know what else "A" is for? A is for ACCIDENT!! Now, pipe down or you're going to find out what "B" is for! I'll give you a hint, "B" is for Butt whooping'!"

Jokes aside, this lady really did end up with a sweet story she can share with her daughter in the years to come. In the future, though, if she is riding with her daughter and they get pulled over by a police officer for say, a burnt-out tail light or something, if the mom is talking to the cop and the daughter decides to play a joke on her and says, "Mama … "D" is for DRUGS!!," then *that* story might not be as sweet.

By the way, I know the mother in this story and she is an amazing human being and law-abiding citizen who I'm certain would never have to worry about facing that situation. If her daughter ever pulled a stunt like that, though, it's likely she would be grounded for all of "E."

"E" is for Eternity.

If she starts behaving again, though, the mom might cut her some slack and ground her for a lesser E: "E" is also for Eon. In life, we must all learn to be flexible.

*   *   *

Life is a lot like the young child in this story. It seems to throw the craziest things at us when we're least expecting it. Sometimes, we don't know quite how to respond. Life, however, can be quite different from a young, innocent child. Life can be downright mean, cruel, and at times, pure evil.

As many of us have long since come to find out, in life, "A" is seldom for apples or "B" for bananas. "C" is rarely for cash bonuses or "D" for dream jobs, either. Many times, "A" is for agony. "B" is for betrayal. "C" is for catastrophe.

"D" is for death.

After awhile, you're grateful there are only twenty-six letters in the alphabet.

Thankfully, God is far more powerful than *anything* life throws at us. God created life, and He and only He alone has the final say. With life, "A" may be for "agony," but with God, "A" is for acceptance and the assurance of knowing He is with us *every* step of the way. With God,

"B" is for blessings. "C" is for compassion. Every letter of God's alphabet stands for something special, especially the letter "J."

"J" is for Jesus Christ.

Perhaps if more of us weren't so concerned about getting a few extra "ZZZZZZ" in bed or even in church on Sunday morning, we would remember that.

As you read this book, you'll see that life has thrown quite a bit my way over the last few years and rarely has it been a bowl of ice cream. We all know the old saying that laughter is the best medicine. It even says in the Bible that "a merry heart" is as good as medicine. Sometimes, though, there is no laughter and our hearts just aren't that merry, no matter how desperately we want it to be.

Going through life is often like trying to find something fun to watch on TV after a long day. All you want to do is just forget your troubles for awhile and watch something that is laugh-out-loud funny. Every show you come to, however, turns out to be cry-out-loud depressing. You watch anyway, though, in the hopes that perhaps, in time, it will get better.

Speaking of which …

Stay Tuned ...
You Might Have Questions!

It's difficult to describe in words just how much I loved television as a kid. As an adult, however, my love affair for television has long since faded away. I can think of plenty of words to describe how I feel about television today, but most of them are questionable, four-letter words that are frowned upon in a book of this nature. Those same words, though, are often held in high regard while stuck in heavy traffic or attending parent/teacher conferences, or so I've been told.

I didn't always love television as a kid. I watched a little TV here and there, but that was it. I actually enjoyed playing outdoors. One day that all changed, though. I remember I was a young child (age, date, and year unknown.). I was in my backyard, playing on the swing set I loved. My mom came to the backdoor and called out, "Brandon, come on in. There's a TV show on you might like!" So, I went in. Within a half hour, I was officially a TV addict and *Fraggle Rock* was my gateway drug. (Looking back, I personally think perhaps there may have been one or two other gateway drugs involved in the production of *Fraggle Rock*, but I couldn't say for sure.)

Growing up, I thought television was amazing. If you were a boy like me, you no doubt watched many of the cop shows with the tough-talking, no-nonsense street cops and their beautiful female partners. As a kid watching these shows, I could never tell if the two cops really "liked" each other, but I learned later on that this was the point of the story line. It was the ol' "Will they or won't they?" scenario. When you're a kid, though, that usually means "Will they or won't they drive their squad car through a crowded indoor mall to chase down a purse snatcher?"

The shows about private investigators were just as much fun. They usually were the smooth-talking, morally-questionable guys who loved the ladies and made their own rules for the sole purpose of being able to come back later and break them.

(Insert inappropriate joke about Congress here.)

Of course, back in the day, we also had an incredible assortment of Saturday morning cartoons to choose from, especially if you were willing to get up early enough. I recall having to be very quiet so I wouldn't wake my parents. I probably could have slept in myself, but then I would have missed waiting for the TV station to come back on the air and hearing them play the national anthem. It felt like it was my patriotic duty to watch cartoons and I was exercising my right to do so.

I loved watching the cartoon shows with talking animals battling the forces of evil in the underworld that threatened to destroy western civilization. I'm sure my parents thought these shows were stupid, but I didn't. I loved these animated characters who saved the day each Saturday. They did all the hard work, and all they ever asked in return was that we watch their shows, eat their breakfast cereals, and purchase just a few thousand dollars worth of all their licensed action figures and play sets. These same cartoon characters also taught us valuable lessons at the end of each episode, like, "Look both ways before crossing the street!," "Don't do drugs!," and "Never talk to strangers!" They also taught us if we were ever in trouble and needed help, it was OK to talk to our parents, our teacher, our minister, a school counselor, a police officer, and even the creepy dude who worked at the toy store who looked like the real-life version of "Comic Book Guy" from *The Simpsons* just as long as he was selling those licensed action figures and play sets from the show. If he was, we were assured he was safe, too.

I even enjoyed watching all the infomercials that used to air back then. Most of them were even dumber than the cartoons I watched, but the products they were pushing were incredible, or so we were led to believe.

Usually how they did it was they had a spokesperson in a room with a studio audience who were *very* easily impressed. They would be trying to sell whatever questionable "as shown on TV" product it was in the most amazing way possible.

For example, if they were selling a car-care product, they might drive a Rolls Royce onto the set, and the host would take a key out of his pocket and just start keying the hood of the car, like it belonged to his ex-girlfriend or something. Then, he would ask his assistant to take some of the product and apply it to the scratches. Within seconds, the key marks were all gone, and the audience went wild. I think we were being introduced to the early days of CGI in those infomercials without even realizing it.

My favorite infomercials were the ones for cosmetics where the host would bring up a young lady wearing the makeup they were promoting. Then they would show how durable the makeup was by showing how well it held up in the rain and extreme heat. When they wheeled out the fire hoses and the flamethrowers, I knew they meant business.

Of course, I can't write about TV of yesteryear without mentioning one of the best things about being a kid back then. It was that glorious week when you turned the TV on and realized you now had ... The Disney Channel!

Now, if I recall, there was a time when The Disney Channel wasn't part of the basic cable lineup. You paid extra for it. For about a week each year, though, The Disney Channel was available to watch. Many children hoped their parents would fork over the extra cash necessary to make The Disney Channel a reality in their homes, but the mindset of many parents was "Enjoy it while you got it." There was a running joke back then that only "the rich kids" got The Disney Channel year round. To put this in context, imagine if *Little House on the Prairie* was set in the 1980s, instead of the 1880s. If so, Nellie Oleson would have been the only kid in Walnut Grove, Minnesota who had The Disney Channel. Down the road at Laura Ingall's little house, they would have no cable, only three channels to choose from, and would still be using a rabbit-ear antenna on top of the roof – with ears from an actual rabbit – that Pa Ingalls shot during a hunting trip. If they couldn't get good reception, they probably sat around and listened to *A Prairie Home Companion* on the radio. If they found out the kids over in "Lake Wobegon," Minnesota had basic cable, it would only add insult to injury.

*   *   *

Without a doubt, my favorite shows to watch during my childhood were sitcoms. I've always loved comedy, and back then, we had great comedy shows to choose from. We had lovable TV families who had funny adventures each week. How these characters got themselves into such crazy situations didn't have to make sense to us, but it made perfect sense in "TV Land." Usually, everything was settled in the funniest way possible by the end of the episode.

However…

Oh yeah, you know where this is headed. You know what I'm about to mention: The dreaded, the feared, the brutal:

"Very Special Episode."

We all remember being subjected to these things. You would be at home in the evening. Your homework was done (well, *almost* done. Okay, you only had to write nine more pages of your ten-page report on the mating ritual of "Our Friend: The Snail," but you convinced your parents that wouldn't take long). You just sat down in your favorite chair with a bag of chips, soda, and the TV remote in your hand. You just tuned into your favorite sitcom, but instead of the usual exterior shot of the TV home with the catchy theme music you've come to know and love, you were instead greeted with one of the actors from the show giving the following announcement:

"Hi, I'm (name of popular 80s/90s TV actor here). On tonight's episode of (name of zany and or/wacky TV family comedy here), we will be discussing (name of whatever currently popular but pressing social issue was deemed necessary to talk about here.) We ask that if your parents are not in the room, please go get them so you can watch together as a family. They may be able to answer any questions you may have. Thanks, and enjoy the show."

Not likely.

Now, I don't know about your home, but in mine, my parents didn't feel like watching a dumb sitcom with me in case I had questions. That was the *last* thing any of us wanted to do. If they did, the conversation would probably go something like this:

Me: "Dad?"

Dad: "Yes, Brandon?"

Me: "I have a question about what we just watched."

Dad: (Reluctant to speak) What's your question, son?"

Me: "I thought sitcoms were supposed to be, well, funny. How come I'm not laughing?"

Dad: "I don't know, son. I don't know."

Me: "Uh, Dad?"

Dad: "Yes, Brandon?"

Me: "Do you realize that if you and Mom weren't so cheap, we could have been watching The Disney Channel right now and this wouldn't have happened?"

Dad: "Go to your room!"

(I wish I *had* been in my room for the last half hour so none of this would have ever happened. I could have been up to the point in my research paper on the snails where the male snail is trying to impress the female snail by saying his family made a fortune selling salt-resistant footwear for the "Snail on the Go," and the female snail is willing to let him buy her a cocktail.)

* * *

I don't know if "very special episodes" on sitcoms are still a thing nowadays, but if so, they're probably *nothing* compared to what they were when I was a kid. Many of us were subjected to "very special" story lines that we will *never* forget. At the time when all those music artists got together and sang, "We Are the World," I think the actors in family sitcoms got together on their own collaboration entitled "Let's Traumatize the Children." Let's look at a few examples of the "very special episode":

The Hogan Family: This was a pretty funny family comedy with typical plot lines from the era, but does anyone remember the "very special house fire" episode? If I recall, the mom character on the show had just died in a car accident. Now, an episode or so later, the family's house catches on fire from an old lamp in the attic. The oldest son, played by Jason Bateman, is coming home from a date and discovers his house is going up in flames. He screams for his family, not knowing if they have all perished in the fire. Thankfully, they're all OK and are soon reunited. As the sad music plays, we see them all standing together as they watch their house burn. They then go to live temporarily with Mrs. Poole from next door. Later on, the family goes back home to inspect the damage, and Bateman's character goes into the charred remains of his bedroom and picks up what's left of a picture frame, which most likely held a now-ruined picture of his recently deceased mother.

Nope, no emotional scarring there.

This episode remains one of the most depressing things I've ever watched. I kept hoping that while the

Hogans were staying with Mrs. Poole, they would discover she had been hiding ALF in her basement or something funny like that, but no such luck. Thankfully, they have great construction crews in the TV universe and by the next episode, the house was completely fixed and life went on as normal.

ALF: Since I just mentioned our favorite Reagan-era space alien, let's talk about him. Remember what would become the series finale when ALF is about to be reunited with his friends from Melmac? Just as he's about to be beamed up in the spacecraft, he's captured by the government agents.

I read once there was talk *ALF* might return for another season. If so, I want to know *how* the show's writers would have gotten him out of this little predicament? I'm guessing they would have just had him wake up in his own bed back on Melmac and exclaim, "Wow, that was the craziest dream *ever!*" (Hey, it worked on *Newhart*.)

Full House: Remember the episode where D.J., the oldest daughter, becomes obsessed with losing weight, stops eating, and is on the verge of developing an eating disorder? Thankfully, her dad sits her down and has that always great heart-to-heart talk with her (with the ever-present musical accompaniment) and within minutes, the problem is solved.

What would have made the ending even better is if Aunt Becky, played by Lori Loughlin (look her up so this next joke makes sense) decides to take everyone out to dinner to celebrate D.J. eating again. It's discovered she needs reservations to get into the restaurant. Becky then bribes the manager of the restaurant to let them all in and another family gets bumped off the list, so it's all good. It's not like she would ever be involved in a restaurant admission's scandal, or anything like that.

Family Matters: This show had episodes that dealt with racism, gun violence, gang violence, and on one episode, Steve Urkel accidentally burned down a restaurant. I'm also *still* waiting to hear whatever happened to the youngest daughter, Judy, who just vanished and has been missing for over thirty years now. I want answers!

There were many more "very special episodes." On *Family Ties*, the son, Michael J. Fox's character, has a friend who dies from injuries from a car accident. He can't handle the death of his friend and ends up in counseling. I read this episode won an award for Outstanding Writing For a Comedy Series, though I can't imagine why. If you're laughing at that, maybe you need a little counseling yourself.

On *Webster*, Webster accidentally burns down his family's apartment with a chemistry set. On *Perfect Strangers*, Larry and Balki and their friends get locked in a flooded basement and they have to escape before the water reaches the circuit box and they all get electrocuted. They end up using an old chemistry set in the basement to blow off the lock and escape. (You know, both *Webster* and *Perfect Strangers* were set in Chicago. I wonder if there was a crossover episode I missed where Webster bought that chemistry set from Larry and Balki at a garage sale? That episode could have won an award for Outstanding *Irony* in a Comedy Series.)

I have to mention *Diff'rent Strokes*. Does anyone remember that "very special episode" where *none* of the main characters got into an accident, developed amnesia, were kidnapped, held hostage, touched inappropriately, bullied, threatened, or had an impromptu visit from Nancy Reagan? Yeah, I don't remember it either.

Also, on the final episode of *Dinosaurs*, they dealt with the consequences of ushering in the Ice Age and facing extinction. And, on *The Cosby Show*, they dealt with the consequences of Bill Cosby. (Personally, I would have felt safer with the Ice Age.)

Punky Brewster: The main reason I wrote this chapter was to have an excuse to write about this show. For those who don't know, *Punky Brewster* was a children's/family comedy back in the Eighties about a girl named Punky who is abandoned by her mom at a shopping center and she, along with her dog Brandon (no relation), end up taking refuge in an empty apartment in Chicago. She is soon discovered by the apartment manager: a grumpy, elderly man named Henry, played by the late George Gaynes. Henry was a photographer by day, and by night, he moonlighted as the Commandant in the *Police Academy* movies.

Punky Brewster was a dark show for kids. First, Punky gets abandoned and has no one to take care of her. She does meet Henry and they grow to love one another, but the government agencies don't think Henry is fit to be a parent. Henry has to fight to get custody of Punky. This was a three-part episode, not a two-part like these types of episodes normally are, so you knew this was going to be an epic battle for the ages.

In another episode, a serial killer is going around Chicago and Punky fears Henry will be his next victim. Another episode dealt with Brandon getting hit by a car and Punky fears she'll lose him. Thankfully, he survives and goes on to live to see the FIVE part episode where

Henry's photography studio burns down, he develops an ulcer and ends up in the hospital, and the government agencies are back again trying to remove Punky from him permanently.

I'll never forget the scene where Punky and Henry are standing in the remains of the burnt-out photography studio. Everything is ruined, and it's as sad as it gets. What I wish they had done was have a special guest appearance by Michael Winslow, the actor who starred with George Gaynes in the *Police Academy* movies who did those *amazing* sounds effects with his mouth. He could have played a firefighter in the background of the scene. Just as Punky and Henry are at their lowest point, he could have made the sound of a smoke alarm and an overhead sprinkler going off. Then he could have said, "Well, better late than never!" That could have added some much-needed levity.

Of course, we can't talk about *Punky Brewster* without discussing what is perhaps the most infamous episode. I'm referring to "The CPR" episode, better known as the "Cherie gets locked in the Refrigerator" episode.

Here's how I remember it: During a particularly brutal cold-snap in Chicago (I believe Chicagoans refer to it as "Tuesday"), Punky, along with her best friend Cherie, and a couple of other friends are in the backyard playing a game of hide-and-seek. Everyone scatters, and Cherie decides to hide in an old refrigerator but gets locked inside. She calls for help, but no one hears her. We are left watching the outside of the refrigerator as Cherie screams to be let out.

This was a frightening scene for a kid to watch, not knowing if Cherie would get rescued from the fridge. I'm sure some of us watching had hoped Mr. T would make a special guest appearance and rescue Cherie but he never showed up. Maybe Ricky Schroder got locked in a bank vault over on *Silver Spoons* and he was already on his way to rescue him, who knows.

Eventually, Cherie's friends come back, someone opens the refrigerator, and they discover Cherie's lifeless body. They get her out and perform CPR. Thankfully, she regains consciousness and will live. This episode taught kids and parents alike the importance of knowing how to perform CPR. It's a great lesson, but did they have to teach it in such a disturbing way? I read that the title of the episode was "Cherie Lifesaver," but I think it should have been named "Cherie Icee" instead.

I'll *never* forget the image of poor Cherie in the fridge. I think a lot of kids, now adults, have never forgotten it. I'm sure some kids had nightmares after watching this. I can picture them dreaming about going into their kitchen for a late-night snack, opening the fridge, and seeing Cherie holding up the milk saying, "Don't drink out of the carton!" In that same dream, poor Judy Winslow's picture is on the side of the milk carton because they still haven't found her yet. I'll say it again: I want answers!!!

*   *   *

There's one last "very special episode" of *Punky Brewster* I need to discuss, and it's one that hit *very* close to home for my own family. It was the episode where Punky and her friends are all excited about watching the Challenger Space Shuttle launch. Their teacher lets them watch it in school, just like many kids in real-life were doing on that fateful day.

While the characters on the show were fictional, the events of that day were *very* real. Kids, their teachers, and many other adults watched in horror on that cold, January morning in 1986 when the Challenger Space Shuttle exploded, killing everyone on board, just moments after take-off.

While we never saw a scene in the episode where the kids watched this tragedy unfold, the other scenes showed the horror they felt (we all felt) that day and how they learned to cope with the tragedy. None of us who were alive back then will ever forget that day.

So, *how* did this hit close to home for my family? Well, my parents *knew* one of astronauts who was killed that day, the late Michael Smith. They attended the same high school as Smith. He and my father were in the same graduating class in Beaufort, North Carolina (Class of 1963). At one time, Smith and my dad played on the same junior varsity basketball team. While my father and Michael Smith were never best friends or anything like that, Dad has never had anything unkind to say about him. My parents said that even then, Michael dreamed of flying. He died fulfilling that dream, and my parents will never forget him.

The airport in the Beaufort area now bears Smith's name. Today, many people may not know Michael Smith's name or the names of the other astronauts who perished almost forty years ago, but their sacrifice, courage, and legacy will never be forgotten.

* * *

Life isn't a scripted TV show. None of us truly knows what will happen from one moment to the next. Even if we did know, we don't know how we would handle a certain situation until the moment we come face-to-face with it. Life doesn't work that way. At best, going through life is like being on a never-ending episode of *Whose Line is it Anyway?*

We want to be happy and successful. We want to have endless, crazy adventures just like the characters on our favorite TV shows. However, just like our favorite characters, we'll all eventually encounter "very special episodes" in our own lives. We can't always solve our problems in a half-hour or hour. On TV, they may have a two-part episode if something really bad happens. In real life, it can feel more like a two-hundred or two-*thousand* part episode, with no end in sight.

Thankfully, if we put our trust in God, we can know that our own "very special episodes" will ultimately have a happy ending. That doesn't always make it easier during the middle of the episode, however. If my family thought going through the pain of losing someone they once knew in a tragic accident was bad, it was *nothing* compared to a time not long ago when we faced the first-hand consequences of a global pandemic and multiple health scares, including a health scare so bad a member of my family almost had their own "series finale."

Stay tuned … you might have questions.

The "Very Special Chapter"

(PART ONE)

I'm tired.

I'm tired, overwhelmed and underappreciated, overworked and underemployed, in over my head and under everyone's feet.

I feel like the proverbial rubber band, you know, the one that's about to break? Well, I "broke" a long time ago and all I want to do is to just lie here quietly but can't because I've been picked up by someone who has decided to use me as a shoelace because their old one wore out and they can't afford a new one, thanks to inflation. That's life. The world is the shoe, and no matter how desperately I want to stop and get off, it just keeps moving forward with me in tow.

There are many words that can aptly describe the last few years. On that very long list, I can almost guarantee that the words "toe-tapping," will not appear. "Toe-stubbing," on the other hand, would appear and be an appropriate description. Also, many of the words one uses when stubbing a toe would also be on that list. The year 2023 was more of a "toe-severing" year for me, but I'm getting ahead of myself.

I remember sitting in my house in the days leading up to the start of the new decade and thinking, *2020 is going to be the BEST YEAR EVER!!!* I would soon come to realize that God hadn't blessed me with the gift of prophecy.

We all know what's happened in the world over the last few years. For me, the world as I once knew it started unraveling around Christmas of 2019. I was casually reading an article online about a new virus that had popped up in China, which, as we all know, would later be named COVID-19. Even though at the time it was believed the virus was only in China, I felt it was my duty to keep informed of such matters. I mean, this was right up there with the Presidential election or Taylor Swift getting a haircut.

Now, I am the dictionary definition of a germ freak and a hypochondriac. If someone coughs on me, I go into full-blown, five-alarm, *Midnight in the Garden of Good and Evil* mode. As soon as I have access to the internet, I will research all the possible diseases I may have been exposed to which I soon learn may include a cold, the flu, COVID-19, the Freshmen 15, *Adam-12*, RSV, RSVP, R-E-S-P-E-C-T, COPD, LADP, NYPD,

Defund the PD (that one always proves to be fatal), yellow fever, scarlet fever, spring fever, *Saturday Night Fever*, chickenpox, Shingles, storm gutters, HMPV, MPV, MSG, SUV, and possibly an airborne form of postmenopausal osteoporosis known to attack men in their forties. (Hey, I read it happened to a guy in Ohio. Look it up.)

When I read the article about the virus, I felt I must sound the alarm and warn my family. My mom, being my mom, tried to reassure me everything was fine. Here's the synopsis of what she said that day as well as in the following weeks:

Week 1: "Brandon, the virus is over in China. That's thousands of miles away. We're fine."

Week 2: "Brandon, I know the virus is getting worse in China, but it's still thousands of miles away. We're fine."

Week 3: "Brandon, I know the virus is now sweeping through Asia, but it's still nowhere near us. We're fine."

Week 4: "Brandon, I know they just had their first case of the virus in Washington state, but that's on the West Coast and we're in North Carolina, so we're fine."

Week 5: "Brandon, I know we just had our first case of the virus in North Carolina, but that was several counties over, so we're fine."

By March of 2020, when the world was going on global lockdowns and church choirs everywhere were starting their final in-person services with renditions of "It's the End of the World as We Know It," even Mom had to admit, "Maybe we're *not* fine."

*　　*　　*

We all remember the lockdowns. We remember those early days of people flocking to Walmart, Sam's Club, Costco, Target, Trader Joe's (or for those of us who live in military communities – G.I. Joe's) among many others to stock up on "needed" supplies. Back then, there seemed to be two burning questions: 1.) Are we going to get sick? And 2.) Are we going to run out of toilet paper? (Many of us feared the outcome of the second question more than the first one.)

I recall the impromptu "DIY" movement that occurred at this time when people spent countless days in their homes making two ply toilet paper out of dryer sheets and duct tape. It had to be two ply because (and this is just my personal opinion) single ply toilet paper is worse than having no toilet paper at all. We do use single ply toilet paper in my home, but only in the guest bathroom to discourage potential overnight visitors. So far, this has proven successful.

Of course, we also have to talk about how hand sanitizer had become the equivalent of liquid gold. By the start of the pandemic, the little bottle of sanitizer I always carried in my pocket gave me a sense of power and prestige I had never before felt. Had I not been so concerned about social distancing, I could have used the contents in that little bottle to attract potential girlfriends. I think some people actually did and were successful. To this day, I still believe Purell should have changed the official name of their sanitizer to "Love Potion No. 9."

During those first months of the pandemic, my family was worried we would run out of toiletries and groceries, so we, like many others, stocked up. We bought what we could, but respected the limits of how much of each item could be bought. Dad started going out early in the morning to shop during the designated "senior shopping hours." A couple hours later, he would return home with the back of our Honda Pilot loaded down with that week's supplies. Before anything was brought into the house, it was thoroughly disinfected. The number of disinfectant wipes we went through was astonishing. We learned through trial and error about when an item is clean enough. For example, if you're wiping down a box of Fruit Loops and by the time you're done, you look down and all you see is the "oops," you can scale back a bit on the cleaning.

Since there was only so much space in our kitchen pantry, Dad started leaving most of the groceries in the garage. They started out stacked on tables but soon, it got too cluttered so he bought and assembled two portable shelving units right in the garage next to the car. It became a running joke in my house that if we were looking for something in the kitchen pantry and couldn't find it, we were told to check on "Aisle One, next to 'Automotive.'"

Of course, when you buy that much food, you have to cook it. Like many Americans at that time, we felt the best way to do this was in a newly purchased air fryer. It's hard to put into words America's love affair with the air fryer during the pandemic, but it essentially became the lava lamp of the COVID generation. When my parents first brought it, they were ecstatic. When it arrived, you would have thought they had just bought the Ark of the Covenant on Amazon. I'll admit, though, the meals they cooked in the air fryer were pretty amazing: all *three* of them.

Now, just like the above-mentioned lava lamp, the air fryer just sits there enjoying an early retirement. It serves as a reminder of what was, and what never will be. It's sort of like my love life, but without the "what was" part.

* * *

Despite countless people losing their jobs and businesses shutting down, I still held onto my job as a gas station attendant. I had become an "essential worker." I wish I could have been an essential "remote" worker, but sadly, it's difficult for gas station attendants to telecommute.

So, there I was at work, in all my "essentiality," ready to serve my customers as always. It was rough. Customers were frustrated with everything that was going on in the world. Sometimes, they were downright mean. There were days I came into work feeling like James Dean in *Rebel Without a Cause* and left feeling felt like Barney Fife in *Deputy Without a Bullet*.

During this time, I took what precautions I could. I started wearing my trusted face mask. I won't lie, it had its advantages. I felt safer with it on when I had to get very close to a customer. For an added bonus, if the customer was getting on my last nerve, I could smirk and stick my tongue out at them and they were none the wiser. My one regret is that during this time it didn't become more socially acceptable to wear oven mitts so I could make questionable hand gestures to annoying customers and they could be none the wiser, either.

During the pandemic, we did what we could to keep our customers safe and healthy. When I came to work, I had a spray bottle of blue liquid at my disposal and was told to spray it on the gas pumps throughout the day to disinfect them. To this day, I still don't know what was in that bottle. I could have been spraying a combination of blue Kool-Aid and Smurf snot for all I knew. After months of this routine, I was hoping by Christmas, Santa Claus would bring every licensed driver in America a new Tesla so that all of us exhausted gas station attendants could just call it a day.

By the way, if anyone reading this happens to work for Tesla or any other EV company, if you're looking for an official mascot, I would like to throw my name out there. I think a gas station attendant would be a great choice! I can see the commercials now: Scores of EV's on the road and one lone gas station attendant (yours truly) sitting by himself at a deserted gas station looking miserable. It'd be great. I could be the next Maytag repairman or Chick-fil-A cow. Let's make this happen!

* * *

The year 2020 was a *rough* year. Because of all the health and safety precautions, I didn't get to be with my friends like I wanted to do so badly. Had it not been for the virus, I would have been taking day trips with long-time friends to the nearby coast, eating seafood together, and sharing the same stories of our teenage years we've heard a gazillion times before but never get old despite how old we're getting. However, none of that would be happening anytime soon.

There was a joke going around at the time that all we had to do was stay at home and watch Netflix. So, that's what we did. My parents and I binge watched the first three seasons of *Stranger Things*. Personally, I didn't find the show all that frightening. I've been in the Baptist church my entire life and after you've seen the outcome of the senior adult ladies being told they have to move out of their Sunday School classroom so the younger married couples can have it, Demogorgons aren't all that scary.

*　*　*

COVID wasn't the only bad thing that happened to me and my family in 2020. During the first few months of the pandemic, the decision was made to demolish the fellowship hall at my church. The building was originally constructed in the early sixties. It was a two-story brick building that housed our sanctuary, the church office, as well as Sunday School classrooms on the first floor. The second floor also contained additional classrooms. After the completion of our new sanctuary in 1990, the "old" sanctuary was converted into our "new" fellowship hall. For almost sixty years, the building was used to feed those who hungered both spiritually and physically.

I fondly remember growing up in that building. I attended Sunday School classes there until the age of fourteen when we switched classes into a new building that has just been built on the opposite side of our current sanctuary. I remember back in Sunday School when I was six-years-old, we were all given brand new Bibles. The Bible had a shiny black cover and I brought it with me to church for years until it fell apart. I miss that old Bible. After Sunday School was over, I would walk down the hall to the sanctuary. Soon, it would be time for the morning worship service to start. I remember being a young child and sitting with my parents during the service in the "old" sanctuary. I recall how hard and uncomfortable the pews were. They didn't have padding like our pews have now. Being so little it was hard for me to concentrate on the sermon, so my parents let me draw during the sermon to keep me still. I would sit on the floor and quietly sketch away with a pencil and paper on the seat of that hard pew. It was a good drawin' pew even if it wasn't a good sittin' pew.

In later years, after the building became our fellowship hall, we had many delicious meals there. I remember our Wednesday night suppers before prayer meeting. I would usually try to be one of the first ones in the food line, if not *the* first. I was often successful in my endeavors.

I'll never forget the time we had just gotten a new lady to head up our hospitality committee, the committee that helped organize the Wednesday suppers. She tried to change things around, which is never a good move in a Baptist church. One Wednesday, instead of having everybody get in line at once, she assigned each table a number. When the number was called at random, that's when the people sitting at that particular table would then get in line. I won't go into graphic details about the outcome, but she ended up resigning within about ten minutes. The moral: If you give a Baptist a number and tell them when to come up, your number will soon be up, too.

I remember in later years attending the church's annual Valentine's Day dinner in the fellowship hall. We called it a "Friendship Banquet" because we didn't want the widows in the church to feel left out, so all the adults were invited. When I became a Sunday School teacher, I always attended the Sunday School teacher appreciation dinners held there in the summer. Even my parents' fiftieth wedding anniversary reception was held in that fellowship hall.

As the years went by, the condition of the fellowship hall began to deteriorate. Many storms, including hurricanes, came through the area. Even after the storms were long gone, the damage that had been done to the building remained. The roof was now in bad shape and mold was a concern. From what I understand, many of the Sunday School classrooms upstairs were no longer in use, either.

A decision had to be made: repair the building and get it back into shape or demolish it and completely start over. We had just begun discussing what to do when the pandemic began. Instead of meeting together to vote on the future of the fellowship hall, each church member received a ballot in the mail. I voted to repair it, as did the rest of my family. Sadly, we were outvoted.

In recent years, many new families had joined the church who just didn't have the same emotional or spiritual connection to the fellowship hall that many of us long-timers had. To many of them, it was just an old, worn out building. To many of us, though, the building was so much more.

Demolition began in the coming months. Due to the pandemic, my family and I weren't attending church during the time of the demolition. I couldn't bear to watch it happen, anyway. I couldn't tell you if the church ever held a special service to "say goodbye" to the building, but I hope they did something. If a prisoner about to face execution gets a last meal, shouldn't a fellowship hall about to be demolished get a "last meal," too? Looking back, I regret not sneaking onto the demolition site at night and taking one of the bricks from the rubble and keeping it to remind me of what once was.

It's been four years since the fellowship hall was torn down. The church is currently looking into converting the old parsonage into space for a new fellowship hall. Only time will tell what the final outcome will be.

If you're new to the area, you would never know there had been a building on the spot where our fellowship hall once proudly stood. I know it was there, though, and miss it terribly. I've often thought about the former members of the church, those founding members who voted to construct that building over sixty years ago. I wonder what they would think if they knew it had been torn down. We'll never know, though. Once you pass away, you can't vote to save old fellowship halls, though

I've heard rumors you can still vote in Presidential elections.

*   *   *

Speaking of those who are no longer with us, this book wouldn't be complete without mentioning one of my favorite people of all time. I'm referring to my former pastor, Dr. Murphy.

Dr. Murphy proudly served as the pastor of my church for over ten years but had long since retired. He passed away during the first few months of the pandemic, but from what I understand, it wasn't from COVID. He died around the age of ninety. I hadn't seen Dr. Murphy in several years but had heard his health was failing. His wife of many years passed away not long before he did. From what I heard, he was ready to go. My family didn't attend the funeral because of the possible risks. I heard the turnout could have been better. Had it not been for the pandemic, I'm certain it would have been.

During Dr. Murphy's life, he taught college religion courses for many years. After retiring, he was called to preach at our church. Dr. Murphy loved people. He encouraged his congregation to love people. Dr. Murphy's philosophy was: If life gives you a lemon, thank "life" for giving you the lemon and invite it to church on Sunday. Whether it was a handshake or a hug, a college recommendation or a character witness, a job recommendation or perhaps even a job, Dr. Murphy did what he could for his congregation and the surrounding community.

I remember going on weekly church visitation with Dr. Murphy. He was determined to make contact with as many visitors to the church as possible, even if we got lost along the way. Trust me when I say we commonly got lost along the way. That was OK though, because Dr. Murphy's other philosophy was: The shortest distance from Point A to Point B is through a cornfield, a golf course, or an artillery range.

To this day, I think of Dr. Murphy often. I was proud to call him my pastor and friend. I only hope he would be proud of me in what I accomplished in my life. Have I done enough? Probably not. Have I make mistakes? More than I care to admit. Regardless, I know Dr. Murphy would have never stopped loving and caring about me.

Rest in peace, Dr. Murphy. It may have been years since you stood in that special place behind the pulpit, but you have *never* left that special place inside my heart.

*   *   *

Time marched forward, and 2020 turned into 2021. My family and I had all survived the first year of the pandemic.

Sadly, so many others hadn't been as fortunate. Then, at the start of the year, my father started having severe back pain. It got to the point he had trouble walking. He started using a walking stick just to get around the house. Dad decided he needed to see the doctor, who, in turn, ordered tests. The preliminary tests didn't reveal what was causing the back pain, but they did reveal something *much* worse: Dad had Leukemia.

I'll never forget the day we found out. I was angry. We had done everything we could do to survive the pandemic for *this* to happen? When it comes to personal health, however, I've come to believe whatever doesn't kill allows something else the chance.

We persevered, though. Dad was blessed with an outstanding oncologist (the same one who helped my mother through her Lymphoma cancer battle years earlier). Dad started a chemo pill regimen twice daily. Thankfully, he has responded very well despite the fact the treatment has impacted his immune system. Since then, we have all had to be even more careful about staying healthy. We started taking advantage of online delivery and curbside pickup services. I thank God that such services are available. I thank Him even more that Dad is still with us.

*   *   *

Soon enough, 2021 rolled into 2022. We were all still together. Dad's chemo pill regimen was going well. His back pain was getting better, too, thanks to medication, cortisone injections, and physical therapy. However, by late September, my entire family still managed to get COVID. Despite all our precautions, the illness still found its way into our home. My sister came down with it first. Soon, my mother got it. Several days later, Dad and I were next in line.

Of course, before our doctor could prescribe the right medication, we had to make sure it was COVID. We were instructed to get tested. Now, some families go on car trips to get ice cream, eat in the car, and wait for the brain freeze to kick into high gear. My family, however, goes on car trips to a COVID testing site to sit in a parking lot and wait for someone dressed like an extra in the movie "Outbreak" to come up to our window and stick the world's longest Q-tip up our noses to see what's lurking up in there.

Does everyone remember back in the good ol' days (2019 and before) when someone said "You're positive," and you were like, "Yeah, I've been working on my attitude lately. Thanks for noticing." Not anymore.

The week we all had COVID was a lousy week. At times, the only thing that kept my mind off the sore throat were the fever and chills. I remember on the first day I was sick the only thing that made me feel better was taking a long, hot shower. I remember standing in the shower and thinking, *I don't care if we have to pawn the family silverware to pay the next water bill, I'm not coming out!*

Of course, when you have COVID, food doesn't taste like it should. Many people lost their sense of taste and smell. That's not the worst thing that can happen, though. Say you have leftovers in the fridge at the time you get COVID. Maybe it's that Lima bean and Brussels sprout casserole you've been putting off finishing. Well, now since you can't smell or taste it, now is the best time to eat it. Plus, this gives your gag reflex a few days off so it can recover, too.

Thankfully, between the antiviral medication we were prescribed and the fact we were all previously vaccinated, the virus ran its course relatively quickly. Mom and Dad still had to take an extra round of antibiotics for a sinus infection, though. I had to deal with "COVID cough" for almost a month. I hated whenever I had to speak to someone and I would start coughing. I thought it would never stop, no matter how hard I tried to stifle it. I had this fear that I would be at work and a co-worker would ask me, "How do you like my new haircut?," and I would say, "It looks great!" Then, just as they turned to walk away, a cough would come out and they would turn back to me and say, "And what does *that* mean? You *don't* like my haircut?" Then, I would have to smooth things over and assure them I *did* like their haircut. This would be followed by yet *another* cough. By now, they would be accusing me of being a liar and me accusing them of being overly dramatic. One thing would lead to another and co-workers would start taking sides, managers would get involved, and paperwork would be filed, all because of a cough. I then envisioned myself standing in line at the unemployment office wishing I had come down with "COVID brain fog" instead so I could forget I ever knew any of these people.

*　*　*

Weeks after recovering from COVID, the holidays were now upon us. Christmas was nice, but uneventful. Mom made her traditional seven-layer Christmas cookies and punch. They tasted as good as always.

Before we knew it, 2022 had rolled into 2023. People were more than ready to move on from the virus. Many already had moved on. My family was still in "2020" mode, however, due to Dad's health issues and the fact he and Mom are in their seventies. We tried to stay optimistic, though. I remember New Year's Day of 2023. I thought, *The worst is over. The best is yet to come!* Sadly, I couldn't have been more wrong.

To Be Continued.

The "Very Special Chapter"

(PART TWO)

A week after New Years, Mom started getting sick. It started with stomach and digestive issues that lasted for several weeks. She took the medicine prescribed for her but nothing seemed to help. It got to the point she was afraid to eat out of fear of what might happen afterward. While Mom's stomach issues eventually settled down, she then developed issues with memory loss. She had trouble forming words and sentences. We thought it could be brain fog issues from Long COVID. We even feared it could be the early stages of Dementia. We would later discover that when she had the stomach issues, her potassium levels dropped, which caused memory loss and heart issues … on top of existing heart issues.

Mom went to her cardiologist in early February. He ran tests. A few days later, she went back to hear her test results. The results were not good. Mom came home in tears. Her heart was in bad shape. More tests would need to be done, but she was told she would likely need a pacemaker installed later that year.

Mom continued having issues forming words. She

also wasn't thinking clearly. We had to watch her to make sure she wasn't taking too little or too much of certain medications.

One night while I was at work, Mom had taken an extra pain pill without anyone's knowledge and was completely "out of it" the rest of the night. After I came home, Mom just sat in her chair and stared at the TV screen while I sat next to her to make sure she didn't try to get up. At one point during the commercial of the show she was "watching," I changed the channel to watch the weather forecast. Then I changed it back to Mom's program several minutes later. She hadn't even realized I had changed the channel.

That night, Dad and I led Mom to bed. Mom, being mom, though, had to still check all the doors to make sure they were locked. She kept fiddling with the handle on the front door over and over. Dad and I had to gently pry her hands off it.

By the end of February, we didn't know how much longer we could keep Mom out of the hospital. On February 27th, I thought I was coming down with a sinus infection. I stayed upstairs to make sure Mom and Dad didn't catch what I thought I had. I talked to Mom (from a distance) maybe two or three times the whole day. She just wasn't herself. Later that night, Mom called up to me from downstairs to tell me she was going to bed. She didn't sound right. I called out, "Good night!" She responded with, "Goodbye!"

The next morning, I woke up to the sound of a siren in the distance getting louder and louder. I still hadn't put two and two together until a few minutes later when I heard people talking downstairs. I quickly got up and looked out the window and saw an ambulance parked in front of the house.

Mom!

I quickly got dressed and went downstairs. The paramedics were getting ready to load Mom into the ambulance. I found out Dad had checked on her a few minutes earlier and saw her lips were turning blue. He called 911.

Dad went with Mom to the hospital. They ran tests, and after looking at the results, the hospital staff thought Mom should be home in a couple days after they got her potassium levels stabilized.

She remained in the hospital for twenty-eight days.

Mom started out in a private, basic care room. She never really understood what was going on around her. She tried to constantly get out of bed, and Dad and my sister had to stop her from hurting herself. Several days in, Mom's heart was in such bad shape that it went into what they refer to as "V-tach" and they had to use the paddles to shock it back to stabilize her. There was talk she would need a feeding tube. There were a lot of tears cried and prayers prayed for Mom that day.

God heard those prayers, and thankfully, Mom made it through the day and started to slowly recover. She wouldn't need the feeding tube after all. Modern medicine is incredible; God is even *more* incredible.

Despite improving somewhat, it was decided Mom needed a higher level of care so she was moved to Intermediate Care. Dad stayed with her most of the time. He slept in the reclining chair next to her bed. My sister and I took turns staying with Mom during the afternoon so Dad could come home and rest.

I remember the nights at home without Mom or Dad. My sister was in and out. I remember sitting in my recliner in the den watching television. Mom and I always watched the same shows together. I often turned to look at my mother's empty recliner next to mine. Sometimes I think I stared at that recliner more than I did the television.

Unfortunately, things took a turn for the worse yet again. One day it was my turn to stay with Mom. I walked into her room. She was asleep and hooked up to a machine of some sort. The nurses had been trying to get her blood pressure regulated. Her kidneys hadn't been functioning properly, either. I quietly sat by her bedside and tried reading a book I had brought. The topic of the book was exploring the world around you on foot so you can better see all there is to see. Oh, how I wish I could have been doing that right then, with Mom walking by my side. Instead I had to read about others doing it, or that's what I would have been doing had I gotten past the second page. The noise from the medical equipment attached to Mom served as a painful reminder that my world right then was confined to these four hospital walls.

An hour or so later, someone from the hospital staff brought dinner in for Mom and me. I had just taken my first bites of rice when a nurse walked in and looked at Mom's numbers on the machine. They weren't good. The decision was made to move her to ICU.

By now, things were starting to move quickly. Before the nurse came back, I had made what phone calls I could make letting my dad and sister know what had happened. Mom was awake, but not really understanding what was happening. I wanted to tell Mom how much I loved her, but knew I couldn't say it without crying. I tried to be brave for her. I tried to make a joke out of it. I told her, "Well, Mom, I thought we were going to have a nice quiet dinner together, but I guess that's not going to happen."

She acted as if she knew what I was talking about. Perhaps she was trying to be brave for me, too.

As Mom was being moved to ICU, a nurse escorted me down through another elevator. She assured me Mom would be well cared for there. I nodded, trying desperately to fight back the tears. When we reached ICU, I was escorted by the nurse to what was referred to as the ICU lounge. I'm sorry, you can call it a lounge all you want, but at the end of the day, it's just another hospital waiting room. And that's what I did: wait. Alone. My mom, only a few rooms away, but not with me. My father and sister, only a few miles away, but still not with me. All I had were my thoughts and my tears to keep me company. I was in *very* bad company.

While in ICU, Mom wasn't allowed overnight visitors so Dad couldn't stay with her. At first, he wanted to sleep in his car in the parking lot of the hospital. My sister and I put a stop to that for obvious safety reasons. When Mom was allowed visitors, we continued taking turns staying with her. One day I was sitting with her alone in the room. They had soft music playing over a speaker and I sat there and watched her. She was asleep so I just tried reading a book I had brought. The title of the first chapter was "It Could Be Worse." I remember thinking unless the title of the second chapter is "But it Will Get a Whole Lot Better," I won't be doing much reading today, either.

At one point during her stay in ICU, Dad received a phone call around three in the morning that Mom had fallen out of bed. I wasn't there so I don't know what happened. I'm not accusing anybody of any wrongdoing. Mom has always been a fall risk. Mom could go on a cruise and fall *out* of the water and *onto* the boat.

I made the mistake, however, of posting on Facebook about Mom's fall. I had friends sending me private messages, going off and saying, "Your family needs to do this!" and "Your family needs to do that!" I wanted to write back and say, "Well, *you* need to HUSH UP!!" It's easy to say what others should do when you have never experienced the same situation. At that moment, I didn't need unsolicited advice; I needed unconditional love.

Thankfully, after a few days in ICU, Mom was moved back to Intermediate Care. A week or so later, they said Mom was *finally* well enough to be released. My father had been with her every day and night, minus the nights she was in ICU. Mom was scared when he wasn't there. At one point, she asked the doctor if Dad could be certified to be her service animal. I'm sure the doctor probably thought she was still "out of it" for saying that. Little did he know that was a positive sign.

On her last day in the hospital, Mom was fitted for and started wearing a Cardiac LifeVest. If you're not familiar with them, basically, it's a medical vest a heart patient wears with wires attached to it that connect to a handheld defibrillator. It detects irregular heartbeats and shocks your heart if necessary. If you walked into a bank wearing one of these things, they might think you were wearing a bomb and everyone would be afraid it that if you didn't get three hundred thousand dollars in tens and twenty's, you would detonate it. Had our medical insurance not paid for most of Mom's medical bills, we might have had to give that idea some serious consideration.

When you wear a LifeVest, you have to make sure all the wires are properly in place. If not, the device may not work when the heart needs to be shocked. I guess my mom was right all along: The wrong kind of wardrobe malfunction *can* be fatal.

It's also important to know how to properly use the LifeVest so the heart doesn't get shocked unnecessarily. Early on, we had a technician come out to the house who showed us which buttons to push on the defibrillator box in case Mom couldn't push them in time. It felt like a demented version of family game night. Instead of playing "Don't Wake Daddy," we were playing "Don't Shock Mama."

Mom *hated* wearing the LifeVest. She was never comfortable with it on her. She even dropped the defibrillator box on her foot on a few occasions. She nicknamed it "Brick." Mom started to treat "Brick" like a person. It was cute at first, but when she started referring to "Brick" as my brother, I put my foot down.

*   *   *

I'll never forget the day Mom finally came home from the hospital. In the hours leading up to her arrival, we had to get the house ready for her. The insurance helped pay for a hospital bed, a walker, and a portable toilet. The portable toilet would save Mom a lot of steps at night. For an added bonus, if we ever threw a formal dinner party and needed an extra chair, we now had it covered.

Mom's first night home didn't go as planned. Around three in the morning, I was awakened to the sound of someone knocking on my bedroom door. It was Dad. He said he needed help getting Mom off the floor. Apparently, he had helped to get her up to use the portable toilet, but in the process she slowly lost her footing and gradually slipped down. He didn't want to wake up my sister, so it was up to the two of us to get Mom up. Mom was OK and hadn't been injured, but neither of us had the strength to pull her up. We were all so tired and Mom was still too weak to help us pull herself up. We finally decided to call 911. Two female emergency workers arrived a few minutes later and couldn't have been nicer. They carefully assessed the situation and soon helped get Mom safely off the floor and back into bed.

We were *not* off to a great start.

During her first weeks home, my father, sister, and I took turns staying with Mom as much as possible. We didn't want to leave her alone. I remember one afternoon we had gotten her ready for a nap in her recliner. I stayed with Mom while Dad worked upstairs on the computer. He had to catch up on a lot of things since he had been with Mom so much in the hospital. By the time he came downstairs to relieve me, Mom was asleep, so I quietly got up from the chair I was sitting in and went upstairs while Dad got settled on the couch just a few feet from where Mom was sleeping so he could take a much-needed nap himself. Things went great for about an hour, when suddenly, from upstairs, I heard Mom shout, "Brandon!" The fear in her voice got me downstairs in a matter of seconds. It turns out Mom hadn't realized Dad was now in the den with her. She didn't see me and thought she was all alone. We assured her we never left her alone and she soon calmed down. Later that day, when I was alone, I started to cry. I thought about my mom fearing she was alone and how, years from now, when Mom and Dad are gone, the fear of my being alone, too.

Thankfully, my sister found an agency that provides personal care assistants for people who are in physical need. By this point, we were *all* in physical need. Through this agency, we met C. I won't share her name for privacy reasons, but we're so grateful God put C in our lives. She was what Mom and all of us needed, at just the right time.

Despite now having C to help us, the next several weeks were still difficult. Mom's heart was very weak. She had little appetite and didn't want to drink much water. Her weight remained very low. We tried to get her to eat and drink more but couldn't force her.

About a month after returning home, Mom started to act strangely. We would ask her if she was OK and she would snap at us. She was constantly paranoid that someone was out to get her, including us. We weren't sure what was going on with her. A couple days later, she even asked me, "Brandon, are you still working at the gas station?"

I hit the roof.

How could Mom not know where I worked? I started asking her random questions and kept getting wrong or nonsensical answers. It took her several tries to even guess my age correctly. I knew something bad was happening. We knew we had to watch Mom very closely.

Early the next morning, Mom had a screaming fit. My father and sister had to calm her down. A couple hours later, though, Dad knocked on my door to ask me to help get Mom up to use the bathroom. She wasn't acting right. She was saying things that made no sense. Honestly, she was hallucinating. She thought people were hurting her when in reality, she was perfectly safe in her own home surrounded by people who wanted to protect her at all cost. When you're a child, you always count on your mom being there to protect you from the invisible monsters under your bed. You never realize that the day may come when you have to protect your mom from the invisible monsters under *her* bed.

Eventually, we got Mom back into bed and calmed her down, but we knew we would be taking her to the hospital in a matter of hours. Later that morning, I sat with Mom as Dad was making plans to leave for the ER. While not hallucinating at this point, Mom just looked so frail. She sat on a chair and I held her hand. I told her we would be taking her to the hospital. I can't even remember if she looked up at me, but she said to me in a scared, childlike voice, "Will you go with me?" I said, "Of course I will."

We drove Mom to the hospital in a town a couple counties over from us because we hadn't been happy with the care she had received at times in the local hospital. They ran tests and she was treated for dehydration. An ER nurse attached an IV bag to her and it started to work its magic. Mom remained there for about twelve hours and returned home early the next morning. It was a horrible experience, but at least Mom now realized she had to do her part to get better. This meant eating and drinking enough not only to survive, but to thrive.

By now, Mom was eating better and drinking more water and now Gatorade to ensure she was getting the Electrolytes she needed. We also kept a closer eye on the programs she was watching on TV. Mom has always loved cop shows, but seeing some of the disturbing images at the time she was dehydrated did nothing to help her mental state. For the next few weeks, we tried making sure she didn't watch anything more violent than a rerun of *Murder, She Wrote*. And, if it was an episode where Mrs. Fletcher left Cabot Cove, we wanted to be in the same room with her.

In case she had questions.

Things weren't perfect, but they seemed to be getting better, at least for awhile.

In early June, I was upstairs using the computer, I heard a loud crash coming from downstairs. I sprinted down the stairs, only to be greeted by the sight of Mom lying on the hard tile floor in our foyer. Dad soon arrived, and within a matter of seconds, we got her up. Mom wasn't hurt, but seeing her lying there was more than I could take. She had seemed to be getting stronger and was walking much better on her own, and we were trying to give her more independence. But just seeing her lying there, all I could do was blame myself for not being there with her to keep her from falling.

A few minutes later, Mom and I were alone in the bathroom, and I lost it. I burst into tears and Mom had to hold and comfort me. I was forty-two years old, but I still needed my mom. Holding her felt so good, but at the same time, it was so painful knowing how close I had come to losing her not that long ago and feared still might.

Several weeks later, around the first day of summer, Mom started acting "off" again. She couldn't think straight. Dad and I had to start walking with her to keep her from falling. She had no appetite. We knew there would soon be another trip to the hospital. I wanted to take her to the ER early the next morning, but there was a problem. Dad had an out-of-town doctor's appointment with his oncologist to do blood work. He needed to make sure he was staying healthy so he could keep doing what he could for Mom. At this time, my sister was out of town, so I called out of work for the day. C, who had now arrived, stayed with Mom and me while Dad went to the appointment. He said to call immediately if we needed him to turn around and come home.

We waited as long as we could, but it got to the point where Mom was in the bathroom, crying. I was crying, too. C, God bless her, stopped and led us in prayer for Mom. That gave us enough courage to keep going. I finally called Dad and he came home. Thankfully, they had just completed his blood work.

Dad and I drove Mom to an ER in yet *another* county because Mom hadn't been happy with the care she got in the second hospital. More tests were run, and the decision was made to transfer Mom to the hospital in that county. I'll never forget when Dad told me the latest test results. It was determined Mom *may* have actually had a heart attack months earlier that none of us, including her, knew about until now. That possible heart attack is most likely what led to all her additional health issues.

When Dad first told me this, I remember thinking, *What have these medical experts been smoking to cause them to take this long to make that diagnosis?* Dad went on to say that it's more common than we realized. He said he heard Willie Nelson had something similar happen to him. I thought, *Well, if Willie's been smoking what I think he's been smoking, I'm not surprised that he wouldn't know if he was having a heart attack.*

While in the hospital (another nearly four-week stay), Mom had a heart stent put in within the first couple days. Just as she was about to have a second stent put in, she fell and hurt her nose. They had to wait for the bleeding to stop before they could put in the next stent. That took days. Most of that time Mom was lying in bed. She began to have issues of delirium. You couldn't have a conversation with her. She would cry "Help! Help!," but couldn't tell anyone how they could help. She would cry out "Mama! Mama!," but her mom was no longer there to help her make sense of any of this. Frankly, at this point, if Mom had said, "Mama! Mama!" followed by, "A is for apple!," we would have been ecstatic.

Mom's delirium continued for days with no end in sight. It was like being in the hospital, the place that was supposed to make her better, was making her worse. One night while I was at work, I just needed to hear Mom's voice. I called Dad on his cellphone and asked to speak to Mom. He put her on the line, but I could tell he did so reluctantly. I told Mom I loved her. She fumbled with her words but did manage to say "love" to me. I want to believe that she was trying to say she loved me, too. After I hung up, I started crying right there in the middle of the gas station. I didn't care what anybody thought.

I prayed every day for Mom. I'll confess that sometimes I wondered if God really heard me. A few days later, though, on a Sunday morning, I was home and got *the* call. It was Dad. He put Mom on the phone. She said, "Hey, Brandon." She sounded wonderful. The tears started flowing yet again, but this time, for all the right reasons. God had heard me after all.

Mom had her next heart stent put in a few days later. She was finally released from the hospital in mid-July. It was a slow recovery. She had little energy at first.

We would walk with Mom around the house to help get her strength back, but she was having so much trouble walking that we feared her legs would give out. We soon discovered she was having a bad reaction to a new medication prescribed to her while she was in the hospital. In order to recover, Mom would have to come off it immediately. We also discovered another medication she had been taking was causing issues with yet more delirium, and she would also have to come off that one, too. At times, being around Mom felt like being around a drug addict going through withdrawal.

For several weeks, Mom had constant mood swings and was easily agitated. Certain noises would set her off. She called them her "triggers." Even the sounds of the washer and dryer upset her. We also learned my mom had amassed a far more colorful vocabulary than we ever imagined. She would become very argumentative for no apparent reason. One night, I was upstairs and heard her shout, "No! No! No!" to my father as she banged the legs of her walker on the hardwood floor. Sometimes when she needed to calm down, she would ask me to brush her hair with her little purple hairbrush. That helped us both calm down a bit. Thankfully, in time, the medicine left her system and Mom's behavior started returning to normal. The washing machine was no longer her mortal enemy. She's still not on speaking terms with the dryer, though.

By November, it was time to take her to meet the doctor who would be performing her upcoming pacemaker procedure. The appointment went well, and they set up a time for her procedure. It was to take place on the morning of December 4th.

I should have been excited. After all, we had been eagerly awaiting this procedure for months, and now it was just three weeks away. I wasn't excited, though. I was scared. All I could think about was how years earlier, my grandmother (Mom's mom) had died in the month of December while in the hospital. Then, I thought about my uncle (Mom's brother) who died suddenly in the hospital after a procedure, also in the month of December. The fear that something could happen to my mom during this procedure terrified me. I never shared my fears with her, though, because I didn't want to upset her.

I needed to talk to someone. I messaged a good friend of mine who is the wife of a local pastor. I shared my concerns. I told her about my grandmother and uncle and all the similarities. I was afraid she would think I was nuts.

Instead, she wrote me right back and couldn't have been any kinder. She reassured me that it was OK to be scared. Through her words, she reminded me that God has a special purpose and plan for my mom's life, just as He does my own. She reminded me that while we should pray that God would allow Mom to make it through the procedure, we needed to have faith that no matter what happens, God would be with her, whether that plan was for her to return to her earthly home or to arrive at her new Heavenly home and be reunited with her parents and brother.

December 4th finally arrived. I tried my best to remember my friend's words. I had more peace than I had before, but still not total peace. We decided earlier on that my sister would go to the hospital with Mom and Dad. I was very nervous and didn't want to make Mom anymore nervous than she already was.

That morning, as we helped Mom into the car with "Brick" clinging to her for what we hoped would be the last time, I hugged her a little tighter and told her I loved her more than once. Just in case.

Soon, I was alone. Honestly, that was a blessing. Sometimes we need to be with others and sometimes we need to be with just ourselves, and we *always* need to be with God. That day, I needed a small church service with just me, myself, and I in attendance.

The day wore on. Dad called and said there had been a delay in the surgery. They were waiting for Mom's turn. I talked to Mom on the phone. I did my best to encourage her. This was in God's hands.

Later that evening, Mom returned home with a brand new pacemaker. The procedure had been a complete success. Now that Mom had the pacemaker, she no longer needed to wear "Brick." Soon, my adopted "brother" was boxed up and left the nest for good. I wish him well.

A few days before Christmas, Mom had a follow-up appointment with the surgeon. He, along with two others, made adjustments to Mom's pacemaker using a variety of devices. Mom had been successfully re-calibrated. It was like watching an episode of *The Bionic Woman*, if she was played by Sophia from *The Golden Girls*.

Christmas rolled around a few days later. It was nice, but uneventful. Mom made her traditional seven-layer Christmas cookies and punch like always.

This year, they tasted *better* than ever.

While some days are better than others, Mom continues to grow stronger. At the time I'm writing this, C still helps with Mom's care, and we're all so very grateful for everything she has done for us.

Mom is walking much better on her own now. She still uses her walker, but not as often. A few times we have even misplaced her walker. That used to scare us because that meant we had misplaced Mom, too. (That's a joke. Don't report us to the authorities.) Sadly, Mom still has congestive heart failure, along with kidney issues. We have to be careful about not leaving her alone for too long. She doesn't sleep as well as she once did, and some days she doesn't have much energy. We just let her rest when she can. Some days Mom gets little bursts of energy and then we *really* have to watch her for fear if we turn our backs for just five minutes, she'll have paint brushes strapped to her walker while she stands on her bed trying to use it to paint the ceiling.

Sadly, just as I was about to put this book to rest, Mom had a recent medical test that showed her Lymphoma cancer *may* be showing its butt-ugly head once again. More tests will need to be done before we know the final outcome. God is good, though, and Mom is still with us. That's what truly matters.

*   *   *

When you come close to losing a loved one, it changes you, for better or worse. There are days I still get angry. I know more four-letter words than even my closest friends realize I know. Thankfully, this is an election year so no one seems to notice.

Some days, I still find myself angry with God. One moment I'm thanking Him for allowing Mom to still be with us, and the next, I'm angry with Him for allowing her to go through so much pain.

When I decided to write this book, I hoped I would have many profound insights to share. When I started doing the actual writing, though, I was quickly brought back to reality.

So, what did I learn from this experience? Well, I learned how merciful God truly is. He showed us that mercy when He sent His Son, Jesus Christ, to die for our sins so long ago. Regardless, many of us approach God and say, "Well, what have you done for me in the last five minutes?" Well, just the mere fact that I said some of the things I said to God and a lightning bolt didn't strike me dead shows just how loving and patient God truly is. I didn't deserve that mercy, but received it anyway, and still receive it.

I was reminded that God is with us, no matter what. I will never fully understand why God allows certain things to happen. Maybe some day He will reveal why things happened the way they did. Maybe He won't. Maybe we were never meant to know. Maybe if we did know, we would be so overwhelmed we couldn't handle it. Thankfully, God can easily handle it. He is working things out in our imperfect lives every second of the day in His perfect timing. Many of us struggle to remember that, but we struggle even more when we forget it.

Now that my family and I have come through this crisis, things are more clear. As Christians, we know that if it had been God's appointed time for Mom to leave this Earth, she would go to be with Jesus in Heaven. We want there to be a tomorrow for us and those we love, but sometimes there is no tomorrow. We can't even know for sure if we'll make it through today. Only God knows for sure.

To sum it up, we all have questions, but only God has all the answers. We all have problems, but only God has all the solutions. We all have the sin, but only God has the salvation. I pray those who read who haven't done so already will put their faith and trust in Christ today. There might not be a tomorrow. With that being said, I'll conclude this chapter by saying this:

Number One: I love you, Mom.

Number Two: Thank you, God, for allowing my mom to still be able to read Number One.

Number Three: I'm sorry, God, for not always making *you* my Number One.

Music & Memories

Throughout this book, as well as previous books, I've talked about my love of old TV shows. One thing I never seem to talk much about, though, is my love of music.

I've always had a love for music. As a young kid, I loved the theme songs to many of my favorite cartoons. As an adult, I'm still unashamedly rocking out to the opening themes to *DuckTales* and *Chip and Dale's Rescue Rangers*.

For me, I have less love for certain genres of music but still love certain songs within those genres. I enjoy listening to certain rock songs, even though I'm not a big fan of rock music. I like a few select rap songs, even though I don't really care for rap music. I also like listening to an occasional folk song even though I don't really care for folk music. (Oops, I just realized I said "folk" again. If I keep that up, this book may be banned in portions of Arkansas.)

It's amazing how our musical tastes as a culture have changed over the last few decades. Thirty years ago, if you asked a kid to give an example of classical music, they might answer "Bach." Today, they would probably say "Britney Spears." In a few more years, NSYNC and the Backstreet Boys will probably be touring the nursing home circuit. If you ask someone under thirty to identify New Kids on the Block, they would probably say they were "one of those barber shop groups who sang Doo Wop songs during the Dark Ages when dinosaurs and Pee Wee Herman freely roamed the Earth."

My love for music is so great that I would have started writing this chapter much sooner but I kept falling down one musical rabbit hole after another on YouTube. I'm sure I'm not alone. You start out listening to a little Paula Abdul or Debbie Gibson, but then you see a link to a Phil Collins song that leads you to a David Lee Roth song you haven't heard in years but just have to hear right this very moment.

(Author's note: At this point, I was planning on doing this hilarious joke using the lyrics to Roth's version of "Just a Gigolo," but then I read about music copyrights and legalities and all that good stuff and decided to pass on it for fear of the outcome. The lyrics to "Just a Defendant" are a lot less catchy.)

*   *   *

Music is powerful. Hearing a certain song or melody can evoke feelings of love, hate, forgiveness, revenge, joy, or sorrow. There have been times I've sat in the waiting room in a doctor's office, sick as a dog and hating life, listening to music playing over the overhead speakers. Suddenly, a certain song would come on and I would start tapping my foot to the rhythm and humming along. Soon, I started to feel better. It was almost like it was worth getting sick just to hear that certain song. The music reminded me that while my illness would eventually pass, my love for that song would remain with me forever.

On the other hand, I've had times where even the most beautiful songs got on my everlasting nerves. For those of us who work in retail, Christmas is NOT the most wonderful time of year. After hearing "Angels We Have Heard on High" for the umpteen gazillionth time playing over the overhead speakers, we can't wait until after the holidays so we can start hearing Mr. Mister sing "Broken Wings" once again.

Speaking of Christmas songs, I have to mention Mariah Carey's "All I Want for Christmas is You," a song that has come to strike fear into the hearts and eardrums of its many unwilling listeners in retail stores. I was thirteen when that song came out and was madly in love with Mariah Carey and *had* to have that CD. Thankfully, I listened to that song so much I built up a natural immunity to it.

*   *   *

As I've grown older, I've noticed just how much some of my musical tastes have changed. Pop music, which I once couldn't get enough of, doesn't really appeal to me anymore. Working as a gas station attendant, I can't tell you the number of times I've had someone drive in with their windows rolled down and blasting the most vile, repulsive garbage I have ever heard coming out of their car stereo. At one time in my life, I might have really liked that music. Today, I think those same songs could make the Devil lose his lunch.

I'll confess, though, that whenever someone drives in blasting reggae music, it makes me happy. Reggae music makes me have wonderful visions of walking on a warm, sandy beach in the Caribbean. Of course, then I have a vision of me getting stabbed from behind with a conch shell and becoming the next victim on an episode of *Death in Paradise*, but at least I was at the beach at the time of my passing.

These days, a lot of the music I listen to is instrumental. I'm at an age now where my philosophy to music is "Don't tell me how to feel. Let me decide that for myself!"

In recent years, I have grown to love instrumental jazz music. I can only name two or three jazz musicians and couldn't tell you the title of any jazz song, but I still love it. For many years on my local Public Radio station there was a wonderful program called "An Evening with Tom the Jazzman." I loved his voice and *really* loved the jazz music. This program is where I got my first taste of jazz music. Sadly, the "Jazzman" passed away a few years back from injuries sustained in a car accident. When he left this Earth, I hope he had Jesus in his heart and jazz on his radio.

Sometimes at work, a car will drive in playing a really great instrumental jazz song on the radio. As I listen, I close my eyes and let my mind wander as it guides me to the destination of its own choosing. My mind often takes me to San Francisco. I traveled there years ago and remember how it looked and felt. With my eyes still closed, I picture myself walking alone downtown. It's autumn, after dark, and there's a chill in the air. Driving down the street parallel to me is a group of four heavily-armed men who are also skilled martial artists. That's OK, though, because in this dream, they are my hired security detail because as anyone who has been to San Francisco will tell you, having armed guards near you is the best way to see the city after dark, or high noon for that matter.

I picture myself stopping in front of a tiny downtown cafe. The weather is starting to turn nasty and rain drops have begun to fall. I walk in, and I'm greeted to the sound of instrumental jazz playing softly in the background. I'm the only customer. The music makes me want to sit and stay awhile. I choose a table next to the window and order a hot chocolate and a pastry (Well, two pastries. OK, a box of pastries, but I'm going to share them with the security guys outside in the car, I promise). I begin to stare out the window and watch all the poor souls still outside without umbrellas hurriedly trying to hail a passing taxi to get them safely (and dryly) to their destination. Thankfully, I have arrived at my destination and I'm not planning on going anywhere for a while. At this point, however, I'll usually hear someone blaring down on their car horn. I open my eyes and I'm brought back to the painful reality that I've been at work at the gas station this whole time. What's weird, though, is that I still smell the pastries. Then, I turn around and realize I'm about to be hit by a food truck. Once I'm safe, I want to close my eyes again and go back to where I'm the happiest, but can't. The car with the jazz playing on the radio is long gone. It was a nice trip while it lasted, though, if only in my mind.

*　*　*

Another "jazzy" style of instrumental music I love is Lofi Hip Hop (sometimes called Jazz Hop). It's hard to describe this style of music. It's sort of like jazz for people in their forties who are desperately clinging to their twenties. It's like regular instrumental jazz, but a bit edgier. Had I been discovered listening to this kind of music back when I attended a fundamentalist Baptist high school, I probably would have had to undergo spiritual counseling. Back then, we had to follow a lot of rules such as No Smoking, No Drinking, No Swearing, and No Dancing. I'm pretty sure somewhere on that list was No Lofi Hipping and/or Hopping.

I've heard that listening to Lofi Hip Hop is very popular with high school and college students these days, though. Some even claim it helps them to better concentrate on their studies. (If Jessie on that "very special episode" of *Saved by the Bell* had listened to Lofi Hip Hop, maybe she wouldn't have become addicted to caffeine pills and could have sung "I'm So Excited" with the rest of her friends.)

What's interesting about listening to Lofi Hip Hop or any style of music geared towards a younger audience is how it brings back vivid memories of my teenage years. For me, regular instrumental jazz takes me to where I want to be now, but Lofi Jazz Hop takes me back to where I once was. Sometimes when I listen to a certain Jazz Hop playlist, I'll come to a song and I'm transported in my mind twenty-five years earlier to the night of my high school graduation.

*   *   *

As mentioned earlier, I attended a fundamentalist Baptist high school, and a *small* one at that. There were four seniors in my graduating class, myself included. Trust me when I say that I was more than eager to graduate. You've heard the term "Senioritis"? Well, I contracted that ailment halfway through my freshman year. It was one for the medical journals.

As big a milestone as my graduation was, I'll confess I was so pumped up on adrenaline that night that I can't recall too many details. I remember the graduation was held in the school chapel. My parents and I left home in plenty of time to arrive early. To celebrate the event, Dad drove us there in the classic car we owned back then: a 1970 Cadillac DeVille convertible.

Now, if this had been an episode of a TV show, "very special" or otherwise, the car would have broken down on the way to the graduation. We would then have to sprint to the chapel in order to make it there on time. Since my parents hate running, they would have given up after half a block and told me to go on without them. I would continue running while looking at my watch and end up running into a parked police car. The officer would get out and question me as to what I was doing. I would be talking gibberish so nothing I said would make any sense. He would ask to see my ID, but I would reach into my pocket only to realize I left my wallet at home. He would then come to the conclusion I'm mentally unbalanced (which, honestly, isn't that far from the truth) and put the handcuffs on me and take me to the police station for further questioning. While at the police station, I would be mistakenly identified as a serial polygamist they had been looking for the last six months. I would get my one phone call and call Dad on his cell phone, only to realize he left it on the phone charger at home next to my wallet.

By now, I would be in a holding cell next to a three-hundred pound, tattoo-covered dude who tried to burn down a fast food joint because his chicken wasn't "extra crispy" enough. Thankfully, through the magic of television, the police would realize they made a mistake and I would be released, just in time for my parents, the principal, the school choir, the pianist, as well as the rest of my senior class to arrive and the graduation ceremony would now take place in the jail.

Soon, the pianist would break out a portable keyboard and play "Pomp and Circumstance" while I, along with the rest of the senior class walked down Cell Block Three.

We would give our graduation speeches, be awarded our diplomas, and then the school choir would break out into an impromptu rendition of "Jailhouse Rock." Then, after the graduation was over, all the choir members would be promptly expelled because it was deemed sinful for knowing the lyrics to "Jailhouse Rock."

Because this wasn't a TV show, however, here's what *really* happened: The car never broke down and we made it to the chapel with time to spare. My parents found a seat inside and I, along with the rest of my tiny class, stood in the church office just outside the chapel as we waited to march in together. As we waited, one of us, I can't remember who, said something like, "Well, this is it." Then, another one of us, still can't remember who, said, "Yeah." And ... that's it. Just tugs at your heartstrings, doesn't it?

Moments later, we marched in, found our seats, and the ceremony began. We each gave a short speech, and soon our names were called to receive our diplomas. We then stood next to the principal as he said "If anyone here knows of any reason why this person should not receive this diploma, let them speak now or forever hold their piece." (OK, that didn't happen, but it should happen because it would make graduation ceremonies much more fun for everyone in the audience who doesn't want to be there.)

After receiving our diplomas, everyone applauded, and we sat down to listen to our principal, Mr. Strickland, deliver the commencement address. I couldn't tell you one thing he spoke about that night because my heart was racing. I never thought this night would come. I really thought I would do something that would keep me from graduating. This was a *very* strict school, and if they found out I knew the lyrics to Britney Spear's song, "Baby, One More Time," I feared my time would run out. (By the way, if you're a man in your forties and get caught singing "Baby, One More Time" at work, you may find yourself attending a sexual harassment seminar. Ironically, if you're that same man and they catch you singing Britney's other song, "I'm Not a Girl, Not Yet a Woman," you may end up as the keynote speaker at a diversity and inclusion event.)

Let's get back to the story. So, at the conclusion of the graduation ceremony, we seniors, now new grads, marched out of the chapel and across the parking lot to our school building where a reception honoring our class was held. During the reception, there were countless congratulatory handshakes, hugs, a few parting gifts, and final words of encouragement. For me, most of the words were "Aim low, and you won't be disappointed." They were joking, of course, but ironically, that advice has served me better in life than anything that I missed in the commencement address.

When I look back on the reception, I recall those final moments just before leaving. Most of the crowd had already left, and by now, there were just a few of us remaining. I remember packing up my gifts, saying my final goodbyes to Mr. Strickland and a few remaining staff members, and walking out the double-glass doors in our lobby for what would be the last time. Twelve years as a grade-school student had come down to this moment. The moment I stepped out the door and my feet hit the concrete, it was over. Before now, I would be just walking out into the gravel parking lot. This time, however, I was walking out into *the real world*. I was no longer a student. I was a graduate. A visitor. Technically, I would soon be a trespasser.

In twenty-five years, I have yet to return to my old high school. I've ridden past it a few times but never gotten out and walked around the campus. Just after graduating, Mr. Strickland, along with many other members of his family who worked at the school, resigned from their positions. Issues were going on in the church the school was affiliated with that were just too much for them to take any longer. They soon founded a new school and church that is still going strong with a new generation of young people.

Sadly, I recently read online my old high school had closed. I couldn't say why, but I know student enrollment dropped dramatically after Mr. Strickland and his family left. Honestly, I'm amazed it stayed open as long as it did. They say it's closed temporarily, so I guess there's always a chance it could reopen. Only time will tell.

I'll always be grateful for all the hard work and sacrifices Mr. Strickland and his family made to make our school so great. I haven't spoken to Mr. Strickland in over fifteen years. I keep up with his family on Facebook. I've heard he's been battling health issues for a few years now. If I were to see Mr. Strickland today, I'm not even sure he would remember who I was, but I hope and pray that I never forget him.

* * *

As I was preparing to write this chapter, I tried recalling memories of my middle school and high school days. I thought about journeying to the far, forgotten corners of my attic and blowing off the dust and cobwebs on my old yearbooks to see what I could uncover inside them. While writing my previous books, I referred to those yearbooks countless times. Long story short, apparently, I had referred to them one time too many because I was coming up with nothing more than an allergy attack from all the dust. Since my yearbooks were of no help to me this time, I sat back in my chair and decided on my next strategy. As I was contemplating my next move, suddenly, it hit me:

There was a bag of Oreo cookies in the pantry downstairs!

For me, Oreo's in the stomach are like fuel for the brain. Then, I remembered we also had vanilla ice cream and milk in the fridge. If Oreo's are my Unleaded Fuel, then a vanilla & Oreo milkshake is my Premium fuel.

Later, as I drank/ate my milkshake, I continued to try recalling school memories, but wasn't having much luck. Then, after I had finished my milkshake, I remembered something important:

I'm lactose intolerant.

(Come to think of it, that explains why I later regretted eating those bowls of ice cream back in the first chapter, too.) Without going into too many details, it wasn't long until I sounded like I ran on Diesel fuel. I had to stay on track, though, and soon, it *really* did hit me:

My old scrapbook!

Not long after graduating high school, Mom presented me with a special gift. She had been saving photos, news clippings, and bulletins from the special events of my childhood and teenage years. She had taken the time to put them all in a special scrapbook. It had been years since I had last opened that scrapbook. It had been sitting on a shelf in my bedroom collecting dust just like its yearbook cousins in the attic.

I retrieved the scrapbook and walked back to my recliner. It was heavy and I had to use both hands to carry it. I sat down and opened up the large book. On the first page was a picture of me and my parents sitting at a table in our now-demolished fellowship hall at church. It was the annual Graduate Recognition Breakfast. I had completely forgotten all about this. I shouldn't have been surprised, though. As Baptists, we look for any reason to have a meal. Having graduated from a Baptist school, I'm surprised they didn't present my diploma to me in a casserole dish.

I continued looking through the scrapbook. Soon, a piece of dark green paper caught my eye. I removed it from its clear, protective cover. On the front it read "Christmas Collage" and was dated December of '98. It was the program for the school-wide Christmas program held during my senior year. I couldn't recall a Christmas program that year. I had no recollection of this whatsoever. I sang in the choir the entire time I was there, so I would have been there. Why couldn't I remember? On the program, I found the list of songs the choir sang that night, and the last song was "The Twelve Days of Christmas." How could I possibly forget singing *that* song?

Then, I suddenly remembered: I *was* at that concert and I *did* sing "The Twelve Days of Christmas." Only, it wasn't that particular song. It was a *parody* of "The Twelve Days of Christmas." How could I ever forget how much we Baptists love parody songs. The two go hand-in-hand. It's like Quakers and kickboxing tournaments.

I couldn't tell you why we sang different lyrics. Perhaps the lyrics about "lord's a-leaping" and "ladies dancing" were deemed too "Pentecostal-ish."

It was starting to come back to me, but only in pieces. I recalled different members of the choir sang the different parts of the song, and I was number … ?

FIVE!

I was Number Five, the BEST number in any version of "The Twelve Days of Christmas." Five is always the part of the song that is sung with "flair and elegance," which for a seventeen-year-old guy is translated "loudness and obnoxiousness." How could I ever forget such a beautiful memory from my youth?

Let's see, what did I sing? It's on the tip of my tongue:

"FIVE ….. SOMETHING OF SOMETHING ELLLLSSSSSEEE!"

Yeah, that's it! Let's see, I'm trying to think of the remaining lines. I think it was something like:

Four ... Uh, can't recalls.
Three ... Oh, Don't knows.
Two ... Who really cares?
And ... probably a tree of some kind that bears fruuuiiitttt!" (Probably "the fruit of the spirit" since this was a fundamentalist school.)

Yep, good as nailed it! Looking back, I can't recall if anyone in the audience shouted "Amen!," but I'm certain no one shouted "Encore!"

* * *

I continued flipping through the pages of the scrapbook and found a copy of my high school graduation program. I read all the names of the grads. Since there were only four of us, that took a good three seconds. I did notice for the first time that the two girls in my senior class both had the same middle name. Not exactly a Fox News Alert, but I suppose if someone over at CNN thought it was part of a bigger conspiracy to help re-elect Donald Trump, they might run with the story.

I carefully removed the old program from its protective cover so I could read the inside. I found the page where our school song had been printed out for all of us to sing.

I won't write out the lyrics, but the chorus is based on the verse found in Isaiah 40:31 (KJV) which reads:

"But they that wait upon the LORD shall renew *their* strength; they shall mount up with wings as eagles; they shall run, and not be weary; and they shall walk, and not faint."

The memories were really starting to flood back now. Our high school mascot was an eagle. The male "eagles" played flag football and basketball. The female "eagles" played volleyball and basketball. We had both a boys' and girls' basketball team. If I recall, every boy was automatically on the football team, including me. Due to my poor vision and overall lack of coordination, I didn't get much playing time. However, on the rare occasions I was allowed to play, I didn't really feel like an eagle. If anything, I felt more like a turkey. Specifically, I felt like a turkey on the Thanksgiving episode of *WKRP in Cincinnati.* My running onto the football field was the athletic equivalent to Mr. Carlson throwing those turkeys from the helicopter. Once I was out there, it was too late to turn back. After watching my athletic prowess on display, the spectators were like a bunch of Les Nessman's seeing firsthand the damage that can occur when you drop turkeys onto unsuspecting people.

Oh, the humanity!

I kept flipping through the scrapbook. I found my mom had kept a bunch of my old report cards. Since I've already cried enough while writing this book, I'm going to skip those.

I soon came to the section in the scrapbook where Mom had saved some of the congratulatory cards that people sent to me leading up to graduation. Many of us have memories of receiving such cards. They usually contained a sweet hand-written note from the sender. If you were anything like I was, however, you never read the note because you were too concerned whether or not they had enclosed cash or a check. Once you took out the gift, you felt like your job was done.

For the first time in nearly a quarter of a century, I made the effort to read (*really* read) the messages on those notes. What I discovered almost immediately was that many of these hand-written notes of encouragement and congratulations were from friends and family members who have long since left this Earth.

The first note I read was from a wonderful elderly lady named Ms. Marge who I knew from church for many years. She passed away a few years ago. After rereading the words carefully for the first time in years, I discovered Ms. Marge had actually written a beautiful little poem. I had never noticed before now.

On the next note, I read a sweet message from Ms. Frances, the long-since deceased wife of our long-since deceased minister to senior adults. She wrote that she hoped I would be successful in whatever endeavors I undertake. She lived just long enough to see me become a gas station attendant. (I really hope she didn't get writer's cramp from that note.)

Soon, I noticed two separate cards from former neighbors of mine: the elderly couples who lived next-door as well as across the street. I stopped thinking about old school memories and began thinking about old neighborhood memories.

* * *

The "old" house. My family moved onto our old street in the summer of '74. Seven years later, I came along. I was twenty-three when we moved out of the house and the neighborhood. That was twenty years ago.

I remember our old house wasn't particularly large. It always felt cramped, but in a comfortable way. I remember the magnolia tree in the front yard that my grandfather had planted right after my family moved in. My mom loved that tree. On the rare winter days we got snow here in Eastern North Carolina, that magnolia tree never looked more amazing. It was always fun watching the snow pile up on the large magnolia leaves as I sat in front of the large window in the living room. In the summer, I would climb that magnolia tree, when I was small enough to climb it. In the backyard, there was my swing set and an old shed we used for storage. Dad later built a brand-new, larger shed. He was proud of that shed. When we moved, I think he missed it more than he did the house.

One thing about winters in that house I'll never forget were the times when my grandmother ("Granny") came to stay with us when the weather forecast called for snow. Granny hated being cold. She always was afraid her pipes would freeze up. Whenever she visited, she stayed in the kitchen as much as possible because the heat from the oven felt good to her. It was the only place in the house she ever felt warm. In our current house, my mom's bathroom is the "go to" room for warmth because of the large window in there that feels great when the sun shines through it, especially in the morning. As Mom was recovering from her illness, she became more like Granny because now she really hates being cold, too. She even bought a small space heater we keep on the counter next to her sink in the bathroom. I suggested we name the heater. Since "Brick" was already taken, we settled on the next best thing:

"Brick Oven."

If Granny had lived long enough to see us move into our new home, I know she and Mom would have spent many hours just sitting together in that bathroom in front of "Brick Oven," just letting the sun from that window shine down on their faces. Then, before she went back home, Granny would have tried to swipe "Brick Oven" in her luggage before Mom ever noticed. Mom would have noticed, though, but just let it go.

*　*　*

I can't recall if I ever saw our former neighbors again after we moved. Mom and Dad visited the couple we lived next door to at least once and they caught them up on all the neighborhood happenings. She still sends us a Christmas card. Her husband passed away a couple years back and she now lives in another community. I've heard she still owns the house they lived in on our old street.

I remember very little about the elderly couple from across the street. They both passed away years ago. I do remember the wife drove this beautiful vintage VW Beetle. It was almost identical to one my dad drove for years. Mom used to tell me the neighbor lady wasn't a very good driver. The way she told it was that Beetle spent more time in the gutter than most bowling balls.

What I remember very well was the day of Mom's heart attack (the first one). It was in February of 2004, at pretty much the same day construction had begun on our current home. Mom woke up on a Wednesday morning, feeling sick. She called out of work because she thought she had caught the flu from one of her students at the elementary school where she had worked as a teacher's assistant, just a block over from our old home. She stayed home that day and the following day. At one point she thought she was feeling a bit better.

Then, on Friday morning, Mom took a turn for the worse. Thinking it was still a nasty case of the flu, she made an appointment to see our family doctor. It was in his office later that morning he discovered she was having a heart attack. She was transported to the local hospital and then later transported to another hospital several counties over. They put in a heart stent and by Monday, Mom was back home with us, thank the Lord. (Thank the doctors, too!)

Mom never went back to work. Her heart couldn't take the stress of the job. She went back to the school to clean out her desk but didn't stay long. I think it was hard for her to come to terms with the fact the job she loved so much almost killed her. The last few months we lived in that house, Mom spent the time recovering.

Moving day was bittersweet. We left a lot of memories in that old house. Since moving, at least two families have lived in our former home. The magnolia tree my grandfather planted some fifty years ago was still there the last time we drove past. I never really knew my grandfather. He died when I was only two. I can't remember what it was like to climb into his arms, but in a way, when I climbed onto the strong branches of that magnolia tree, I now realize it was like he was right there with me.

Moving into our new home was a good day. We needed a change. Sadly, a few months later, Mom was diagnosed with Lymphoma. We had wanted a new chapter in our lives, but little did we know what the contents of the chapter would hold. Still, Mom bravely underwent chemotherapy and radiation and was declared cancer free three years later.

We don't go back to the old neighborhood much anymore. So much has happened in our lives since then that Mom told me once it feels like we never even lived there.

Several years after we moved, there was one notable incident on our old street. For whatever reason, someone torched a car parked in the driveway of a home a few doors down from our old house. The fire grew out-of-hand and spread to the house, causing extensive fire and smoke damage. The family who lived there had a litter of pug puppies that were injured. I believe one or two of them perished from injuries from the fire. An arrest was soon made, but the damage had already been done.

Thankfully, this story has a happy ending. Shortly after the fire, the owner of a local furniture store donated furniture to the family that was displaced. He also asked if he could have one of the puppies to give to an employee who loved pugs and needed a dog. The family agreed. His employee, an elderly lady, happens to be a long-time church friend. Receiving that puppy meant the world to her.

The little pug had medical issues due to the fire. He had damage to his eyes from the smoke. My friend spent Heaven-only-knows how much time putting the prescription eye drops in his round little pug eyes. She named the little dog Chance. As time went on, Chance grew stronger and healthier. My friend gave him all the love she could give. When she was at work, he went to the local doggie daycare. At Christmas time whenever she sent us a Christmas card, she would sign her name followed by … "and Chance, the Spoiled Pug."

Chance went on to live many years and had a wonderful life. Sadly, the time came not long ago when Chance's health began to fail, and, like so many beloved dogs before him, Chance crossed over the "Rainbow Bridge." Had it not been for the kindness of her wonderful boss all those years ago, my friend would have missed out on having that special kind of unconditional love that only an animal can give.

My friend recently got a new pug puppy. She named him Lucky. I'm certain he *will* live up to that name.

*   *   *

It's amazing just how many long-forgotten memories can be unlocked simply by looking through an old scrapbook. One memory unlocks another, which in turn, unlocks five more. Soon, those memories are collecting faster than snow on a magnolia leaf or notes from a jazz song playing softly on the radio.

Soon, though, it's time to put the scrapbook back on the shelf. We should never forget our pasts, but we can't live in the past, either. That's hard to do when the past often feels nicer and safer than the present or the possible future.

May we take time to thank God for all the special people He put in our lives all those years ago as well as the ones who remain in our lives today, or who may later come into our lives.

One thing I noticed about my scrapbook were all the extra sleeves for photos and such that remained empty. I think Mom realized that scrapbooks aren't just for old memories, but also for all the ones yet to be made.

And that, as the old saying goes, is music to my ears.

Thank-You Notes

(CONCLUSION)

I have lived in the Southern U.S. my entire life. I *love* the South. I can't imagine living anywhere *but* the South. When I die, it had *better* be in the South. On the day of my funeral, I want the church packed with family and friends and I want the service to be one story after another about my life. The oral tradition of storytelling is held in high regard in the South and must live on even if the people in the stories no longer do.

I also want a full Gospel choir to lead the music at the funeral. The songs performed will also be those held in high regard to us Southerners. This will include "Amazing Grace," "It is Well with My Soul," and the opening theme to *The Dukes of Hazard*. Afterwards, I want a huge reception with a catered meal to include such Southern delicacies as Vienna sausage, potted meat, and moon pies. For beverages, there should be Pepsi, Cheerwine, and RC Cola. Then, when all is said and done, my final wish is to have my ashes scattered in the parking lot of the nearest Buc-ee's.

"Ashes to ashes, Dust to dust. Beaver Nuggets to Beaver Nuggets."

The South is a truly special and unique part of America. Take the weather, for example. Here in the South, we *know* snow is pure evil. Even though it's cold and falls from the sky, we know snow *really* comes from the center of Hell. It's a trick the Devil plays on us every winter, but we're on to his little game. If there is a chance of just a quarter inch of snow falling, we lock ourselves in our homes with our guns loaded and ready just in case some misguided soul tries to break in and steal our six-week bread-and-milk supply.

Shopping in the South is also a unique experience. Many of us have long since adopted the philosophy: Why get dressed up to go to the Walmart at the end of the block when we can just stay in our PJs and shop at one of the four Dollar Generals on either side of our house?

By the time you read this, you'll likely be thinking, *Yeah, but you didn't mention the Dollar General on my roof or the other one down in my basement.*

* * *

One thing about living in the South that is both endearing and annoying is the emphasis placed on politeness and courtesy. Sure, they're important, but we take it to levels unheard of in other parts of the country, or perhaps even the universe.

In the South, we stock up on writing utensils and stationary just in case we need to send someone a polite note at a moment's notice. A Southern driver can be sitting in a traffic jam and they'll notice the driver next to them looking annoyed. It's not out of the realm of possibility that the Southern driver will reach over to their glove compartment, pull out a pen and notepad (personally monogrammed with their initials, of course) and jot down a quick note. Then, they'll use hand-motions to get the other driver to roll down their window so they can fling the note through the window and onto the other driver's lap. The note will likely read, "Thinking of you during this difficult time."

One thing we are *big* on in the South is sending thank-you notes. If you fix us a meal, we send you a thank-you note. If you drive us to a doctor's appointment, we send you a thank-you note. If the meal you fixed for us gave us food poisoning and that's *why* you had to drive us to the doctor, we still send you a thank-you note. (By the way, if that last scenario were to occur, if the thank-you note in question contains the words "Bless Your Heart," that's Southern code for "Watch Your Back."

*   *   *

As you have read throughout this book, the last few years haven't always been the easiest for me and my family. That's been the case with so many others as well. Often times, we have seen the worst in people. That's why I believe that when people go out of their way to help us, we need to take the time to thank them.

During this time, some very special people have been there for me when I *really* needed them the most, and I thought I would write some thank-you notes to them on the following pages. I don't mention them by name or initial, but I think they'll know who they are.

As you read the following pages, ask yourself, *Have I ever written or received a thank-you note like any of these?* If the answer is "yes," you have either truly been blessed by others, have yourself been a blessing to others, or both. Perhaps what you read will give you an idea of how you can help someone now or later on when they need it. Please make sure to keep reading until the end because I have a special message for all of you. I'll be disappointed if you don't, and after all, I did say "please." As we Southerners know, a "please" is just as important as a "thank-you."

* * *

Dear Pastor Friends,

I hope this note finds you all well. I wanted to thank you all for everything you do for our church and have done for my family.

Thanks for being there when we called to ask for help in getting Mom safely up and down the steps in our garage so we could get her in the car to drive her to her doctor's appointments. All of you were always so patient and gentle with her. You led her up and down the steps as tenderly as you would a new Christian being led in or out of the baptismal pool on the day of their baptism. At first, I was afraid you would treat her like a church member who put a dollar in the collection plate during the first Sunday of a tithing campaign when you saw them roll up to church that morning in a new Lexus. Thankfully, that was never the case.

To my worship pastor friend, thanks for getting in touch and asking if you could stop by my house and have lunch with me. It meant so much that you offered to bring over Chick-fil-A, even though we all know that if they ever decide to open on Sundays it could mean the end of your career since the food tastes like Jesus cooked it Himself.

Thanks for allowing me to just sit and enjoy myself for a few minutes. Thanks for letting me talk about all the things that you probably didn't care that much about, especially my love of classic TV shows. I apologize for any nightmares you may have had in the weeks following our detailed discussion of *Punky Brewster.* Thanks for all your encouraging words and giving me those few precious minutes of peace I desperately needed.

Thank you for also bringing over the wonderful homemade chicken dishes when my family was on the church's "meal train" when Mom first got out of the hospital. When someone has been hospitalized, a good home-cooked meal not only can bring back your appetite, but can also change your whole outlook. Your chicken dishes were just as good as anything I have ever eaten at Chick-fil-A. That's saying a lot because I personally think Chick-fil-A only selects chickens that completed divinity school.

Jokes aside, thanks for the impact each of you has made on our church. Thanks for unashamedly sharing the Gospel message of Jesus Christ each week. May God continue to bless you and your families as you continue to bless our family, our church, and our community.

God Bless, Brandon

*   *   *

Dear Work Friend,

I wanted to say thanks for everything you have done to help me over these last few years.

I remember at the start of the pandemic when we were told we had to do temperature checks at the start of our shifts. Many of us waited around the department where you were working at the time for someone to come and take our temperatures. I don't recall any of the people who did this seemed too thrilled to be doing it. You would have thought they had been asked to use a rectal thermometer. Thankfully, that wasn't the case. If so, my last pay raise should have been *a lot* bigger.

I remember I could never figure out how to clock in for work at the computer at your desk. I only knew how to use the time clock upstairs. Thankfully, whenever you were there, you took the time to help me clock in. Because of your help, I was never late for the start of my shift. I truly believe God put you there at just the right time to help me. God has a way of doing that.

I know from conversations we have had over the years how discouraging it has been for you at times. I remember you telling me once how you felt nobody cares anymore. Well, that just isn't true, because *you* care.

You show you care by all the simple acts of kindness you do for others throughout the day. You show you care by taking time to make sure others have what they need to ensure they have a good day. You show you care by simply being *you*.

You have told me in the past how others have treated you at times. You've shared with me about some of the hurtful and unkind things others have said to you. I truly believe that the venom that comes from a hate-filled word is far more deadly than any virus the world has ever known. It makes me both sad and mad at how you've been treated and I wish there was more I could do.

Please know that I do pray for you often. I pray you are treated with the respect you deserve and that God keeps putting good people in your life who will do just that. I pray you always keep pressing forward and never give up. As the old saying goes, the Devil will always *try* to "wrong" all the "rights," but God will *always* "right" all the "wrongs." I'm certain God has used you to right more than a few wrongs! Never forget that and please know I will *never* forget you!

Love, Brandon

*   *   *

Dear "Laughing" Friend,

I wanted to take a few moments to tell you how important you are to me. Thanks for being a wonderful friend and having such a positive attitude, especially over these last few challenging years.

Thanks for always laughing at my jokes and for being my all around "Laugh-O-Meter." It's because of your encouragement that this book is written the way it is so if it turns out lousy then I'll know who to blame.

Seriously, though, thanks for all you have done for me, especially while Mom was in the hospital. There were times I felt so alone, but you always did what you could to make sure I didn't feel alone.

I'll never forget once during this time I came into work and felt like I was going to burst into tears right there in the break room. You took time to listen to me and did your best to calm me down. You told me if I needed to talk I could call you during the shift. You even gave me your extension number, do you remember? Even though I calmed down and didn't need to call, I have never forgotten that simple act of kindness. It made me feel better knowing that if I *did* need to talk, I could count on you.

Thanks for always reminding me that laughter is contagious. The sound of your laughter has brought so much joy to many of us at work. Trying to make you laugh has been one of the highlights of many of our careers.

Of course, there were those times when you couldn't stop laughing and we heard sounds coming out of your mouth we felt weren't natural. Some of the newer employees who didn't know you well became frightened because they thought a family of demons had been unearthed and was trying to escape through your nose and vocal chords. They probably began to wonder if there was an "Exorcisms in the Workplace" training mod they forgot to complete. The rest of us, however, knew that it was just part of the joy that comes from working with you, and you have brought us *a lot* of joy!

Love always, Brandon

* * *

Dear "Encouraging" Friend,

I wanted to tell you how grateful I am for everything you have done for me and my family over this past year.

When Mom first got out of the hospital, she came home with little-to-no appetite. She had a bad experience with the food in the hospital. Specifically, she had to *eat* it. It didn't always agree with her, and her appetite had yet to recover. Her weight went down dramatically and she was just wasting away.

I will always remember the delicious home-cooked meal you made for us. From the moment Mom took her first bite, her appetite started to come back. To hear her say she wanted a little bit more almost made me cry. Thanks for not only taking the time to prepare such a wonderful meal, but for also making sure it was prepared in a healthy way so Mom could enjoy every bite. I truly believe you have the God-given gift of knowing exactly when and how to reach out to others when they need help the most, even if they may be too proud or too afraid to ask for help.

I will always be grateful for all the kind notes you sent me when Mom was in and out of the hospital. In one note, you reminded me that life has many twists and turns. You went on to say that life seems to throw us curve balls when we least expect it.

BUT *then*, you reminded me that through God's grace and His love, we can get through those difficult times. You ended the note with what was perhaps the part that meant the most to me. You wrote that I was in your thoughts and prayers every day. Just knowing that I have friends like you who take the time to not only think about me, but to pray for me, and reach out to me, reminds me just how much God has truly blessed me.

Thanks for so many wonderful years of Christian love and friendship, and I truly hope the note you just read means as much to you as the ones you wrote for me. Your words are special to me, but *you* are even more special!

You friend, Brandon

*   *   *

Dear "Broccoli Soup For the Soul" Friend,

I wanted to say thanks for everything you have done for my family and me over this past year! Even though I had known you for many years, it wasn't until Mom got sick that we truly became friends. I'm sorry it took something as serious as an illness to form a friendship that should have been formed so many years sooner under far better circumstances.

I will never forget how in those first few weeks of Mom's illness and time in the hospital, you let me know that ANY time I needed to talk to not be afraid to call you and you would be there for me as soon as possible.

I remember that fateful Saturday morning when Mom took a turn for the worse and I felt like I was going to lose her. I picked up the phone to call you and you answered right away. I told you what was happening and you asked if I needed you to come over. I said "Yes," and I'm so glad I did.

Within a few minutes, you pulled up in front of my house and we sat on the porch. You allowed me to talk about whatever I needed to talk about in order to help me process everything that was happening. You knew I just needed someone there to listen. Thankfully, Mom started to improve later that day, and I know you and many others lifted up some serious prayers that day. We all did.

Thanks for the wonderful homemade broccoli soup you later prepared for us. After the first spoonful, I was quickly reminded that soup isn't just for the cold, winter months; it's good *all* year round! Normally, I'm not a fan of broccoli, but you prepared it in the best way possible: by drowning it in cheese and showing it no mercy!

Thanks for all you do to serve our church as well. Whether it's singing on the praise team, working with our children in Vacation Bible School, or teaching Sunday School, you seek to serve the Lord every time you're in church. Just as importantly, you seek to serve Him throughout the week as you help meet the needs of others. Through your many acts of kindness, you help strengthen those around you who are hurting.

May God continue to bless you as you continue to seek to bless others!

Love, Brandon

* * *

Dear "Sisters in the Lord, Sisters to Each Other" Friends,

It is hard to put into words how grateful I am for both of you. I remember that Saturday just over a year ago when you came to my house at the same time our other church friend did. I believe you were with her at the tine I called and you knew I needed to be with friends at such a difficult time.

I remember the four of us just sitting out on the front porch in the rocking chairs, just talking. Even though it was early March, the weather was warm with a light breeze. It was like God using the sun to remind us of His warmth and love for all of us.

I will always be grateful for all the times I needed a ride to or from work and you were there for me. I will admit, though, that sometimes if either of you picked me up at night and one of you was sitting quietly in the backseat and I didn't notice you at first, whenever you said "Hello," it would scare the living Bojangles biscuits out of me. Thankfully, after my heart stopped racing and I realized we weren't being carjacked, it was all good!

It's hard to believe it's been several years now since both your parents passed away. They were such wonderful, giving people. I can tell you're both their daughters. I remember hearing stories about when your father served our once small town decades ago as a police officer. Not only was he your protector, but he was *everyone's* protector who called our town their home.

Speaking of home, I'll never forget years ago when I had the opportunity to visit your family home for a church event. I can't recall what the occasion was, but I'll *never* forget that amazing view of the lake next to the house. Even though we were right in the middle of town, that lake and the trees that surrounded it made it feel like we were miles away out in the country. The reflection of the moon that night as it illuminated over the water was breathtaking.

I'll never forget how sad I was when that sinkhole formed near the house and the lake was drained due to safety concerns. Considering the sordid past of our town, I fully expected the work crews to uncover multiple rusted-out Packards and Studebakers with the skeletal remains of rum runners and other assorted local legends alike sitting in the front seats. That never happened, though, much to the surprise of many of us. I'm sure your dad was hoping some of the cold cases he may have worked on years earlier were about to be solved, but no such luck.

I will *never* forget how much your father loved Elvis Presley. It's not every Baptist Church that can say they had their very own "in-house" Elvis impersonator. I remember all the great stories about him dressing up like Elvis and entertaining the folks at the local nursing homes. If they had let him, I'm certain your dad would have been thrilled to lead the Sunday morning worship dressed like "The King" as we worshiped the one *true* King. After all, Elvis did perform a lot of Gospel songs. The question is, though, would your dad have just done Elvis' Gospel songs? The last time I checked, "Whole Lotta Shakin' Goin' On" wasn't in the Baptist Hymnal.

I'll never forget when your dad asked my dad to drive him in the annual town Christmas parade all those years ago back when we still had our old Cadillac convertible. I'll *never* forget seeing him in full Elvis attire as Dad drove him with the top down. The crowd loved seeing your dad! That was such a wonderful day.

Even though your parents have gone to be with the Lord in Heaven, you both still carry on their legacy in all that you do for others. I loved it when your dad used to bake cakes for his church friends on their birthdays. Whenever any of us had a birthday, we always wondered if we would get a surprise visit and perhaps be serenaded with an Elvis tune. He made a lot of birthdays a little bit brighter! Whenever either of you show up at my front door with a surprise cake for my birthday, I know it would make your dad so proud you're helping to keep the tradition alive. I can always feel his presence and his love shining through both of you. I feel your mom's love and presence as well.

As you read these words, please know how much I will always love you both and your family. You're all such a special and unique group of people. If there were more people in the world like your family, this dark world would be a lot brighter and a *lot* more fun! Take care, God bless, and thanks for always reminding me about what your father taught us all about how we should treat one another:

"Don't Be Cruel."

God bless, Brandon

*   *   *

Dear Facebook Friend,

I wanted to say thanks for being there for me during such a bad time in my life. Even though it's been many years since we last saw one another, you were there for me when Mom was sick. Our friendship is proof that social media, when used the right way, can be a wonderful thing.

I knew I could message you anytime I needed to talk (or vent). You often responded within a few minutes, if that long. You listened to what I had to say. You didn't tell me what I needed to do. You knew my feelings were valid and that it was OK to feel however I felt. I know you lost your mom sometime ago and I'm sure through that tragedy, it made you more understanding of the pain I felt when I feared I would lose mine.

I know the day will come when you will be reunited with your mom in Heaven, and I know she would be so very proud of everything you have accomplished in your life over these last few years. She lives on through you and I know you show your children the same love she showed you. From what you shared on Facebook, your mom sounds like a remarkable lady who raised a remarkable daughter. I'm very proud to call her daughter *my* friend!

Love, Brandon

*   *   *

Dear School Friend,

I wanted to thank you for the kindness you showed me during my mom's illness. At the time, we hadn't seen each other for nearly a decade. You live so far away and are so busy with work and raising a family. Regardless, you took the time to call and check on me during an especially difficult time where things could have gone in either direction with Mom's health.

I remember being on the phone with you, crying my eyes out. I was apologizing for crying and you assured me there was nothing to be sorry for. You just patiently listened as I cried. I will always be grateful for that simple act of love.

Thanks for reminding me that it's OK to cry, even if you're a man. I honestly believe that if more men were encouraged to cry, this world would be a better place. When we keep our feelings bottled up, they can explode at a moment's notice. When that happens, we not only hurt ourselves, but we also hurt those around us, including those we love.

I'm so glad God put you in my life all those years ago and I'm even more glad we've remained friends. I pray for you and your family regularly. Please know despite the distance, if you're ever in trouble, I'll find a way to be there for you. Remember, I used to help you with your homework, so you know I'll *always* have an answer!

Love, Brandon

*   *   *

Dear Family Friend,

We are truly grateful for all the kindness you and your family have shown to us. We will *always* be grateful for all of the wonderful side dishes you were kind enough to prepare for us at Easter, Thanksgiving, and Christmas. For many years, Mom has done most of the cooking, but this past year, she didn't have the strength. Had I tried to cook, Mom would have ended up back in the hospital along with the rest of us to keep her company. We are beyond grateful for all the delicious casseroles and desserts you, your mom, and sister made for us. You made sure we had delicious food and that made our holidays so much more relaxing and peaceful. We will always be grateful for your kindness and friendship. We pray God's blessings on all of you *all* year round!

Love, Brandon

* * *

Dear College Friend,

I wanted to tell you how much it meant to me that you took the time to come visit me when Mom was in the hospital. It was just one day before Mom went into ICU, so that should tell you what her condition was like. You didn't have a lot of time to sit and chat, but I'm grateful for those few precious moments on my front porch when we just talked and caught up. It's hard to believe it had been five years since we last saw one another. I wish we lived closer and I especially wish I could drive so I could visit you more often.

I know the last few years have been hard since your divorce. I can't even imagine how hard it is to be a single parent. When we talk on the phone and you tell me some of the "horror" stories, I want to sympathize and say, "I know how you feel." I can't though, because I don't know how you feel.

I know there have been personal struggles you have shared with me privately over these last few years. Please know I value our friendship so much, and what you have shared with me *will* stay between you and me.

You are such a wonderful mother. I've seen firsthand how much you love your children, and they are beyond blessed to have you as their mom. You try so hard to meet their needs and I'm sure more than once that has meant sacrificing your own wants.

I'm so grateful God put you in my life all those years ago. When we first sat across from each other in our college business courses, I never dreamed we would remain friends for two decades and counting!

Please know that not a day goes by that I don't pray for you. I pray God continues to bless you and your children. I also pray God blesses you with a Godly man who you can share your life with and loves you and your children as much as you all love him. If by the time you're reading this you are married to such a man, well, God heard my prayers and you're welcome!

All jokes aside, please know I'll always try to be the best friend I can be to you, even from a distance. If you're ever in town, though, please be sure to stop in for a visit. There will always be a place for you in my home and in my heart.

God bless, Brandon

*   *   *

Dear Church Friend,

I wanted to take a moment to write and thank you for all the times you were willing to drive me to or from work while Mom was in the hospital and Dad couldn't be there to drive me himself.

I remember even before Mom was sick, you told us that if I ever needed a ride to please let you know. I honestly believe God was preparing your heart for service even before that service was needed. God knew what I would need at the appointed time.

While it may not seem like a big deal, the fact you helped get me to and from my job was a *very* big deal. I always enjoyed getting to talk with you as we rode together. You had mentioned other friends who you have given rides to when they needed them. You are living proof that not all ministries happen within the walls of a church.

I know the last few years haven't been easy for you. I can't even begin to imagine how hard it was for you when you lost your daughter to such a cruel act of violence all those years ago. I can't imagine how you have dealt, and still deal, with the pain of losing a child, especially in such a horrible manner.

It would have been very easy to allow the pain in your heart to consume and destroy you. I'm so grateful that even in your darkest hour, you still held steadfast to your faith in the Lord. I know God was always by your side, even if you couldn't see Him there. He gave you a desire to help those in need, and you do this in so many wonderful ways, including in your job working with older adults who need love and companionship. You make a positive difference in the lives of others every time you get in your car and drive to your appointed destination.

I'm reminded of that song title by the Grateful Dead, "Keep On Truckin." I don't know if you can do that very easily in your Honda Accord, but I know you can "live 'according' to God's word, and you truly do!

Take care and God bless!

Love, Brandon

*   *   *

Dear Praying Friend,

I wanted to say thanks for all the kindness you showed me while Mom was in the hospital, even though I never saw you once that entire time. Thanks for all your encouraging e-mails. More importantly, thanks for being one of the biggest "prayer warriors" for my family. When I called and updated you on Mom, you didn't just say you would pray and leave it at that. You organized one of the BEST prayer chains *ever*! You relayed my messages and had fellow Christians all over the country praying for my mom. When Mom found out we had people in ALASKA praying for us, she was blown away! (I only hope the people in Alaska weren't *blown away* before they could finish praying for us!)

Jokes aside, thanks for all you do for others. I also want to say thanks for sending us all the beautiful poems you have written through the years. Mom especially loves your poems. She has shared many of them with the ladies in her Sunday School class. You have a special gift for words and those words have brought so much joy to so many.

Thanks for reminding me just how powerful our words and prayers truly are. Physical wars are fought with guns and other earthly weapons, but spiritual wars are fought with an even more powerful, Heavenly weapon: our heartfelt prayers to God. When it comes to prayer, you, my friend, are a Five-Star General!

God bless, Brandon

*   *   *

Dear Sunday School Teacher Friend,

I wanted to let you know how truly grateful I am for all the kindness you showed to me and my family during Mom's illness.

It has been a pleasure getting to help teach Sunday School along with you for so many years. When I first came into our class nearly twenty years ago, I was almost certainly the youngest one there. If you recall, the church was struggling at the time and most of the people from my former Sunday School class had already left. I was one of the few younger members left. I never felt much peace or love in that former class anyway. I felt like most of the people in there would have been happier had I been the one to leave and never return.

When I joined your class, however, I received the love and stability I desperately needed. I would never have guessed that in just a few months, I would be asked to help teach our class. It has truly been an honor.

Thanks for all you have done to humbly and patiently teach God's Word, and that includes all your hard work during the week to prepare for the lesson. I have missed teaching, or just simply being in our class during this past year. I sincerely hope by the time you read this, I will have returned.

I'll always be grateful for the times you got in touch over this past year and asked if we wanted you to bring over some food. You knew that there are times when it's just as important to feed a hurting soul physically as it is spiritually. Sometimes all it takes is a stack of blueberry pancakes from Cracker Barrel to do just that!

In the time I've been away, it's helped me to realize how much I truly enjoy teaching Sunday School. Yes, there have been weeks where I found it difficult to study the lesson plan. Sometimes the lesson was on a difficult subject and I had to read over the lesson over and over again just to learn the basic points. On weeks where we were studying the Book of Revelation, I'm pretty sure I was on my knees begging Jesus to come back on Saturday night so I didn't have to teach about it on Sunday morning.

Regardless, I know I always got the most out of the lessons on the weeks when I was teaching. Through all your hard work, you taught me that when a teacher is ill-prepared to teach, it's not only disrespectful to the people sitting in that class, but also disrespectful to God. Through your example, you help to remind me that we come to church to grow in our walk with the Lord, *not* to be entertained. Thanks for helping me to better understand that.

I'm so grateful you allowed me to teach on the Sunday just before Mom first went into the hospital. Neither of us knew at the time what an emotional week that would be, but God knew. Through teaching that lesson, God helped prepare me for what lay ahead.

In case you don't recall, the lesson that week was on John 11, where Jesus raised his friend Lazarus from the dead. As I was preparing to teach the lesson, there was one Bible verse in the story I kept coming back to multiple times. It was John 11:35, the shortest verse in the Bible: "Jesus wept."

As I taught the lesson that week, I didn't know just how much weeping I would be doing in the days and weeks ahead. Knowing, however, that Jesus Christ, God the Son, who died for our sins, wept for his friend, gave me a sense of peace. It was like Jesus speaking to my heart saying that if He can cry, I can cry, too. Jesus had a LOT on his plate back then. We think we have a stressful life. What we are going through is *nothing* compared to what Jesus was going through back then, especially leading up to His crucifixion. Jesus walked this Earth as both fully human and fully God. He had feelings and emotions, just like the rest of us. Since Jesus never sinned but still cried, I guess that means crying is *not* a sin. And now, the Bible *confirms* it.

Case closed.

I know the last few years have been an emotional time for you and your family as well. I know how much all of you grieved as you mourned the loss of your wonderful wife who was sick for so long. I'm very glad I had the opportunity to help teach our class when you couldn't be there because you made the wise decision to remain at home with her during her final months. Over this past year, I'm certain you have returned the favor ten fold.

Thanks for all you continue to do to help build and grow our Sunday School class, our church, and most importantly, the kingdom of God.

In Christ, Brandon

*   *   *

Dear Neighbor Friend,

Words can't begin to describe how grateful we are for everything you have done for us! We will always be grateful for all the times you volunteered to stay with Mom and keep her company while Dad picked me up from work. I know Mom has always looked forward to getting to spend time with you. Whenever the two of you get together, she always loves hearing all the latest news from around the neighborhood. Mom feels like she is "in the know" now. She no longer feels the whole world has moved on without her, and that's been so good for her.

Thanks for all you do to help out around the neighborhood. Whether it's walking a neighbor's dog, passing out Halloween candy on our behalf, offering me a ride to or from work, or whatever needs to be done, you're one of the first ones to volunteer.

Thanks for your positive "can-do" attitude and your continued friendship!

Love, Brandon

*   *   *

Dear Doctor, Nurse, & Home Health Friends,

I don't know how often the family members of your current or former patients take the time to write you. After everything you all did for us during our time of need, I wanted to make sure *I* took the time. When we were at our lowest point and feared we were about to lose a precious member of our family, God put each of you in our lives when we needed you and your talents the most.

God has given each of you special gifts and abilities and the desire to provide the care needed for those who are sick. Being sick or having a loved one who is sick is very difficult. Often times, you see your patients and their families at the most painful time in their lives. Sometimes, no matter how hard you work to care for your patients, you get treated poorly. I can't begin to imagine the level of stress and pressure you deal with on a daily basis. I saw some of that first-hand during my mother's multiple stays in the hospital.

Still, many of you became our "rocks" when we were on *very* shaky ground. I'll never forget the story my sister shared when Mom was first admitted into the hospital. Mom was so agitated and couldn't think clearly. She didn't want to stay in bed. My father and sister were constantly having to do what they could to keep her from hurting herself.

At one point, there were a couple of young student nurses who came into her room to assist. They were Godsends. They did what they could to help Mom and had good attitudes on top of it. One of them even gave my sister a much-needed hug.

Another time, a wonderful nurse took extra time out of his day to help Mom out of bed and walk with her up and down the hallway of her floor so she could get some exercise. Getting Mom out of bed was one of the best things that could have happened for her, and that nurse made it happen.

I won't lie. There were times when I grew frustrated. There were times when I was with Mom in her hospital room and she needed to use the bathroom or needed some other kind of assistance and I would push the call button on her bed and ask for help. Sometimes, it took much longer than I would have liked for someone to arrive. However, now that I've seen just how many patients you deal with at once, I better understand why we had to wait. You were doing the best you could with the resources you had. This is why it's so important all of you have the proper resources you need to best help your patients.

Of course, the doctors played a major role in Mom's care, too. There were times where we got frustrated while we had to wait for one doctor to confer with another one before a decision could be made about how to help Mom. We now better realize it's not that you didn't care, but you had to make sure your decisions would help Mom and not cause her to have another setback.

Perhaps the best example of a doctor doing the best job possible was when Mom was admitted to the hospital for the third time. She spent so much time in bed she developed what I've heard referred to as "hospital induced delirium." I'm not even sure Mom knew who her family was. One doctor in particular listened very carefully to our concerns and did what she could to find a solution. She made sure Mom received the medication needed to help her come out of it. When I talked to Mom on the phone that wonderful Sunday morning and heard her clearly say the words, "Hey, Brandon," I knew we had turned a corner and were now moving forward.

I also have to mention all the wonderful medical personnel affiliated with Home Health. You all play such an important role in ensuring those under your care receive the care they need while they recover at home. To the physical therapy team who helped Mom regain her ability to walk again, you are angels on Earth. To the physical therapist who worked with Mom the most (and I pray you are reading this), THANK YOU. You took the time to show Mom how to do the leg exercises needed to get her legs strengthened. You showed her the best ways to get in and out of a chair, and how we could safely walk with Mom to keep her from falling.

I'll never forget when Mom first came home from the hospital. She was absolutely terrified of the possibility of walking down the steps in the garage. I even saw her cry and scream about the possibility of walking down them once, though that wasn't when you were there. When you were there, however, you lovingly and patiently showed Mom the safest way to walk up and down those steps. You helped give her the confidence she needed. Today, she walks up and down them with little problem, though we always stay close to her just in case.

Whatever your job in the medical profession may be, through your combined efforts, you each do your part to help ensure your patients regain what they have lost due to illness: their strength, peace, determination, hope, and so much more.

I pray you all know how important your hard work means to so many people, whether or not those people ever say thanks. I'm saying thanks, however, and so does my whole family, especially Mom. Because she can now say "Love you," to me, I can say "Thank you" to the rest of you for giving her back the ability to do just that.

God Bless, Brandon

*   *   *

Dear Reader Friends,

Thanks to all of you who took the time to read this book. For those familiar with my books, I'm sure you realize this book was far more serious than my previous ones. For some, that may have been a turn off. When you read a book from an author who writes comedy, it's a pretty good assumption you're looking to laugh, not cry. Sometimes in life, though, there are far more tears than there is laughter. That's true in the life of a comedy writer, too.

Always remember this, though: When we experience those times of tears when it seems like there is no hope, if we have God in our lives, there is *always* hope. Those tears, as painful as they are, can help us grow stronger. They can make us a better person. They can even help us to better recognize when others are hurting so we can be there for them, just as they were there for us.

With each book I write, there is always that nagging question: Will this book be the last one? Honestly, I don't know the answer to that yet. Writing this book took a lot out of me. Perhaps reading it took a lot out of you.

Regardless, I felt this was a book that needed to be written. For whatever reason, God put the desire on my heart to write these words. Maybe it was to help me through my ongoing healing process. Perhaps it was meant to help someone else in their healing process. Perhaps *you* are that person. Only God knows for sure.

I'll conclude this book by making this promise to all of you: By the time you read these words, I will have said a special prayer for *every* one of you. I might not know you personally or know what you're going through, but I have prayed for you. Everyone needs and deserves someone praying for them. I have done that for you and I hope you'll do the same for others.

May God continue to bless you all, and, as Cherie might say if she still finds time to hang out in the fridge once in awhile: "Thanks for stopping by. Take care, and I'll leave the light on for ya."

Acknowledgments

I can't conclude a book without acknowledging all the sources I used to help make it possible. So, in case you had questions … *now* you have answers.

A FUSCO - Classic TV, "The Hogan Family - House Fire – Burned Out." YouTube. 1 February 2024. Wed. 7 Feb. 2024.

A FUSCO - Classic TV, "THE HOGAN FAMILY -The Hogans Move into Mrs. Poole's House after a House Fire." YouTube. 1 Feb. 2024. Wed. 7 Feb. 2024.

Fitzgerald, Eddie & Sandy Wall, "Popular radio show host killed in Sunday crash," North Carolina Central University, 90.7 JAZZ, WNCU, https://www.wncu.org/music-news/popular-radio-show-host-killed-in-Sunday-crash/, Originally published on www.newbernsj.com. (The New Bern Sun Journal). Feb. 13, 2024.

The Holy Bible, Authorized King James Version, RED-LETTER EDITION, THOMAS NELSON, Nashville, Tennessee, 2017.

The Student Bible, New International Version, With Notes by Philip Yancey and Tim Stafford, Zondervan Publishing House, Grand Rapids, Michigan, 1992.

Wikipedia Contributors. "List of *Punky Brewster* episodes." *Wikipedia, The Free Encyclopedia.* Wikipedia, The Free Encyclopedia, February, 2024. Last edited 5 October 2023. Wednesday 7 February 2024.

Wikipedia Contributors. "List of songs recorded by Elvis Presley." *Wikipedia, The Free Encyclopedia.* Wikipedia, The Free Encyclopedia, February, 2024. Last edited 2 January, 2024. Tuesday 13 February 2024.

Wikipedia Contributors. "List of *Family Ties* episodes." Wikipedia, The Free Encyclopedia. Wikipedia, The Free Encyclopedia, March, 2024. Last edited 7 March, 2024. Tuesday 12 March. 2024.

Printed in the United States
by Baker & Taylor Publisher Services